Ninety Miles

To my family

Ninety Miles

Cuban Journeys in the Age of Castro

IAN MICHAEL JAMES

ROWMAN & LITTLEFIELD PUBLISHERS, INC.
Lanham • Boulder • New York • Toronto • Plymouth, UK

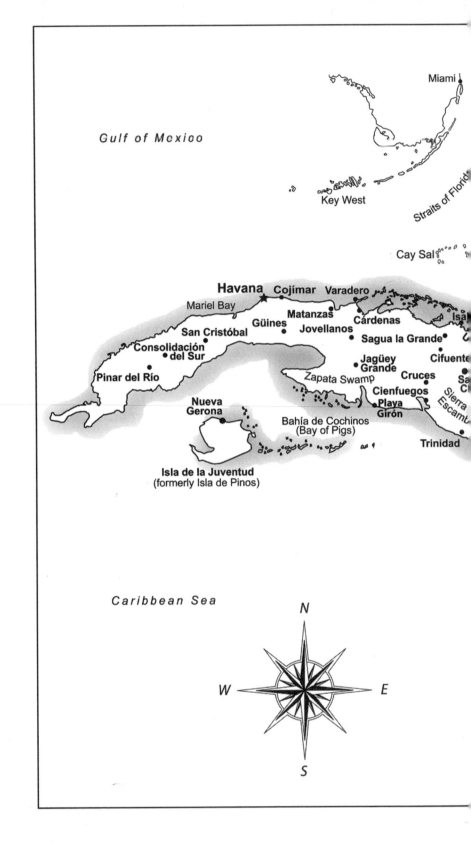

Atlantic Ocean

Nassau

Williams Island

Andros Island

BAHAMAS

Sagua

Caibarién

C

Morón

Sancti Spíritus

ego de Avila

U

Nuevitas

Camagüey

B

Banes

Las Tunas · Holguín

Moa

Santa Cruz
del Sur

Bayamo

A

Baracoa

Manzanillo

Santiago
de Cuba

Guantánamo

Niquero

Sierra Maestra

Guantánamo Bay
U.S. Naval Base

| 0 | 50 | 100 Miles |
| 0 | 80 | 160 Km |

Cartography by Rosa Aray

ROWMAN & LITTLEFIELD PUBLISHERS, INC.

Published in the United States of America
by Rowman & Littlefield Publishers, Inc.
A wholly owned subsidiary of The Rowman & Littlefield Publishing Group, Inc.
4501 Forbes Boulevard, Suite 200, Lanham, Maryland 20706
www.rowmanlittlefield.com

Estover Road, Plymouth PL6 7PY, United Kingdom

Distributed by NATIONAL BOOK NETWORK

British Library Cataloguing in Publication Information Available

Library of Congress Cataloging-in-Publication Data

James, Ian Michael, 1972–
　Ninety miles : Cuban journeys in the age of Castro / Ian Michael James.
　　p.　cm.
　Includes bibliographical references and index.
　ISBN-13: 978-0-7425-4042-2 (cloth : alk. paper)
　ISBN-10: 0-7425-4042-1 (cloth : alk. paper)
　　1. Gutiérrez Menoyo, Eloy.　2. D'Rivera, Paquito, 1948–　3. Lledes, Nancy, 1962–　4. Cuba—History—1959–　5. Exiles—Cuba—Biography.　I. Title.
F1788.22.A2J36　2006
972.9106'40922—dc22
[B]
　　　　　　　　　　　　　　　　　　　　　　　　　　　　　　　2006010910

Printed in the United States of America

∞ ™ The paper used in this publication meets the minimum requirements of American National Standard for Information Sciences—Permanence of Paper for Printed Library Materials, ANSI/NISO Z39.48-1992.

Contents

Preface

These are the stories of three people whose life journeys evolved alongside Fidel Castro's revolution in Cuba. Each of them chose a dramatically different path, and together they tell a wide-ranging human history that spans five decades of life in Cuba and in exile.

Eloy Gutiérrez Menoyo was a rebel commander who once fought on the same side with Castro but eventually turned against him. He spent years in Cuban prisons, and upon his release began to advocate dialogue with his old enemy despite their deep differences.

Nancy Lledes was a child of the revolution who never imagined leaving Cuba until she fell in love with a man who opposed the system. For his sake, she abandoned her country along with thousands who took to the seas in homemade boats and rafts.

Paquito D'Rivera was one of the island's brightest musicians, a leading saxophonist whose high-profile defection shocked Cuba and helped catapult him to world stardom. He was separated from his family for years, building a bitter grudge against Castro.

I began this project seven years ago, wanting to learn more about their lives and the personal struggles that some Cubans have endured. I had just begun working as a reporter in Miami, and was struck by the range of experiences and views within the Cuban community. I happened to meet Nancy and began talking with her now and then about what it was like growing up in Cuba. About the same time, I introduced myself to Eloy after reading about his historic role in the revolution and his uncommon stance in believing reconciliation was possible and necessary.

I learned about the hostility created by the stark political divide between Cuba and the United States, and the trauma suffered by Cubans separated from their families and homeland due to politics, economics, or circumstance.

When in 1998 I joined dozens of Cubans on a flight to Havana—my first—it felt like we were crossing an emotional no-man's-land. Some passengers chatted nervously about the prospect of meeting relatives they hadn't seen for much of their lives. Cheers burst out when the island appeared below, dotted with royal palm trees. Inside the airport terminal, some of the Cubans wept as they spotted relatives and shouted out to them. People fell into deep embraces, smiling through their tears.

Out on Havana's streets, signs with slogans like "Socialism or Death" stood as monuments to Castro's revolution. Some Cubans complained to me that life on the island was a constant struggle, while others blamed the U.S. embargo for their troubles and said they were proud to be living in a socialist Cuba.

I returned from that brief visit believing there was an important story to be told about Cubans' personal experiences. I wanted to tell about how Castro's enduring influence had shaped lives, and to capture some of the human stories of an age filled with upheaval, bitterness, and yet hope.

Living in New York in 1999, I met Paquito and was intrigued by his rambunctious personality, his soulful music, and his dramatic and emotion-filled story of choosing to defect. I decided to weave together the stories of Paquito, Nancy, and Eloy because they represented three generations and three distinct experiences, though all within the segment of Cubans who have found themselves at odds with Castro or his system.

My purpose was not to judge the successes or failures of Castro's rule, nor to claim that the people whose stories are told here represent all Cubans. I chose to focus on three people who for various reasons found faults in Cuba's system, in part because I believed each offered an important and insightful critique. At the same time, I sought to honor the perspectives of those such as Nancy's parents who have wholeheartedly supported Castro and who still live in Cuba.

After Nancy, Paquito, and Eloy shared many hours with me recalling past experiences, I returned to Cuba on longer visits to meet their families and friends and to see the places they described. I traveled through the mountains where Eloy led rebel troops and toured the fort overlooking Havana where he was later held prisoner. I stopped by the music school where Paquito once climbed trees, and attended the cabaret Tropicana, where he was captivated by bands performing under the stars. I visited with Nancy's parents, who warmly welcomed me and shared their mixed feelings about their daughter's life on the other side of the Florida Straits.

Together, the lives of Eloy, Nancy, and Paquito tell a story of suffering and triumph, of coping and courage, of loneliness and love. This is their story, and it is an honor for me to tell it.

1

Havana 1959

All across the city, people heard clanging church bells, blaring car horns, and celebratory gunfire. At last, Fidel Castro and his rebel army had arrived, and Havana celebrated the triumph of the revolution. It was January 8, 1959.

Men, women, and children filled the streets to welcome the bearded rebels arriving from the east in columns of trucks, tanks, cars, and jeeps. The men in battle-worn fatigues riding atop the dusty vehicles waved to the cheering crowds while holding their rifles pointed skyward. Confetti floated in the air, and revelers waved Cuban flags alongside the small black-and-red banners of the main rebel movement. Castro stood in an open jeep, smiling and stretching a hand into the crowd while people shouted: "¡Viva Fidel!"

The crowd parted before Cuba's new liberator. Some put up hand-lettered signs on their front doors that read, "Fidel, this is your house." Others compared him to Christ—a man of the people sent to save Cuba from oppression and free it once and for all.

When he stepped atop a platform and took the microphone that night, tens of thousands of people stood waiting to hear him speak about the rebellion that a week before had ousted President Fulgencio Batista and forced him to flee the island.

"Tyranny has been overthrown. Our happiness is tremendous, but nonetheless much remains to be done still. Let us not deceive ourselves in believing that what lies ahead will all be easy. Perhaps all that lies ahead will be more difficult."[1]

Castro described his vision of a revolution based on pure ideals, untainted by ambition. "The worst enemies the revolution can face," he said, "are the revolutionaries themselves."[2]

"The people are unconquerable, and it was the people who won this war," Castro continued, "because we had no army, we had no fleet, we had no tanks, we had no planes, we had no heavy guns, we had no military academies or recruiting and training teams. We had neither divisions nor regiments nor companies nor platoons, but we have the confidence of the people, and with this alone we were able to win the battle for liberty. The people have won this war."[3]

The crowd responded with a roar of applause that filled the military headquarters at Havana's Camp Columbia. As he ended his speech, a number of white doves were released and flew toward the night sky. One returned and settled on Castro's shoulder. It was as if the heavens had chosen him to speak for Cuba.

Eloy Gutiérrez Menoyo stood listening to the speech next to other rebel leaders. The twenty-four-year-old commander still wore the beard he had grown leading his own rebel army in the mountains of the Sierra del Escambray. Independent of Castro's chain of command, Eloy had been chief of the Second National Front of the Escambray, guiding his men through the forested peaks to drive out Batista's forces.

Standing in front of the cheering crowd, Eloy was filled with joy. Just before the speech, he had finally met Castro for the first time. They had embraced, and Castro welcomed him warmly: "I've really wanted to meet you. Hey, but you're so young. I thought you'd be older."

Eloy smiled. He felt proud and hopeful about the revolution he had helped to create. This was the happiest time of his life.

Paquito D'Rivera was ten years old at the time when the rebels arrived in Havana. As he watched their caravans roll through his neighborhood in the suburb of Marianao, it seemed to his astonished eyes that a gigantic party had touched down on his quiet avenue. He had never seen anything like it.

Paquito would sometimes play in the yard with toy guns, but he had little interest in becoming one of these real soldiers who passed in the street. His heroes were the musicians he listened to on his father's RCA record player, and his parents encouraged him to play the saxophone. By age ten, his life revolved around music. He appeared on television, per-

Eloy, wearing the black jacket, poses next to Fidel Castro at the triumph of the revolution in 1959. (Courtesy of the Gutiérrez Menoyo family)

formed wearing a white dinner jacket and bow tie, and had already traveled to the Dominican Republic and Puerto Rico for concerts.

Before the revolution, Cuba offered Paquito plenty of opportunities. But his parents felt uncertain about the future, and they had little admiration for the rebel fighters or their revolution.

East of Havana in the small town of Sagua la Grande, telephone operator Nancy Espinosa Vergara slipped out of her house to take a walk as soon as she learned of the rebels' triumph. Wearing a dress the color of tobacco, she strolled slowly along the sidewalk, absorbed in thought while a crowd celebrated around her. Tears clouded her eyes as she recalled friends killed in the fight against Batista, but at the same time she felt hopeful that the revolution would bring her country a different, more just future.

A few years later, she gave birth to her first daughter and named her Nancy Ester Lledes Espinosa. A child of the revolution, Nancy grew up steeped in the principles her mother cherished—equality and sacrifice for the common good. As a little girl, Nancy learned to discern the sweet scent of sugarcane carried by the breeze from the fields surrounding Sagua la Grande. She began her school days pledging to be a good socialist, and she cried tears of solidarity when Castro's speeches touched something inside her.

When Castro's rebels rolled into Havana in 1959, the Cuban revolution was just beginning. In the years that followed, the influence of that revolution spread throughout the island's society, leaving no Cuban untouched. Eloy was imprisoned, accused of turning against the revolution he had fought for so wholeheartedly. Paquito boarded a plane on a one-way trip out of Cuba, leaving behind a wife and son. And a grown Nancy reluctantly decided she had no choice but to abandon the island and the people she loved. In a sea blackened by the night, she feared for her life on a rickety boat as men bailed water to keep it from sinking.

Their journeys began with the euphoria of a triumphant revolution that was to right the wrongs of the past. Eloy Gutiérrez Menoyo shared Castro's vision of a revolution as Cuban as the palm trees—a revolution that was neither communist nor totalitarian, a movement to bring social change and freedom to a people who had suffered under dictatorship.

Castro spoke of noble *campesinos*, of doing away with unemployment and illiteracy, and of eliminating discrimination against blacks and women. In its first year, the government enacted an agrarian reform law that nationalized large sugar plantations and farms, and another law that sought to abolish racial discrimination and for the first time opened many hotels, beaches, night clubs, and restaurants to blacks.[4]

The new leader proclaimed that his revolution was founded upon "the absolute respect for human rights" but defended the swift executions of Batista's henchmen by firing squads. He said those who showed no mercy for the lives of others did not deserve to live.

Cuba would be a new country, Castro said, a place where the people controlled their own destiny. He said elections would be held in the future at the appropriate time.

As the rebels settled into life in Havana, Eloy shaved his beard and joined Fidel in the public spotlight, signing autographs together with him and appearing at press conferences and speeches. In those early days, Eloy didn't know what lay ahead for him. He had left behind his old job as a bartender at the Turf Club, a night spot filled with horse-racing memorabilia, while his sister Mercedita had taken over management of a bar he owned, Eloy's Club, which he had opened to help support his family before setting off for the mountains. Upon his return, the rebels of the Second Front crowded into Eloy's Club, basking in their newfound freedom.

Eloy, who was born in Spain in 1934 and moved to Cuba as a boy, felt a strong bond to his adopted homeland. He still spoke with the tinge of a Spanish accent, but in honor of his role in the revolution, the new government granted him Cuban citizenship.

The biggest influence in Paquito D'Rivera's life was his father, Tito, a saxophonist who ran a small business selling musical instruments and accessories such as clarinet reeds and trumpet valve oil. Tito taught his son to read music at the age of four. On the small soprano saxophone his father gave him, Paquito learned quickly and began performing in public when he was only six.

The family lived a short walk from the cabaret Tropicana, a place as far from politics as one could get. Whenever Tito Rivera went there to meet his musician clients, Paquito went along. A sign at the entrance proclaimed the Tropicana "A Paradise Beneath the Stars." Towering trees fringed the open-air cabaret, showcasing the moon at night. At showtime, musicians took their places near the stage, and mirrors along the walls reflected a kaleidoscope of mingling dancers. In that magical spectacle, Paquito saw a future for himself.

Paquito turned eleven in 1959 and was generally oblivious to the changes sweeping his country. But he did notice when his parents grew worried as they watched Fidel speak on television. Castro seemed to go on forever, and when he finally finished, Paquito's mother, Maura, stood and

Paquito with his father, Tito, at his musical debut, mid-1950s. (Courtesy of
Paquito D'Rivera)

announced, "This guy is worse than the other son of a bitch they got rid of, so we're going to have to get out of here, right away."[5]

Eloy Gutiérrez Menoyo stood with the revolutionary government through tragedies as well as triumphs. When a ship loaded with guns, ammunition, and grenades blew up in Havana harbor on March 4, 1960, the blasts killed scores of people both aboard the French freighter *La Coubre* and on the docks. More than 300 people were wounded. Fidel led the funeral procession, linking arms with a row of revolutionary leaders including Ernesto "Che" Guevara, Eloy, and others. Fidel said the dockside explosions were an act of sabotage and suggested the United States was to blame, though he had no proof.

"Do they want to show us that we can be invaded at any time?" he asked. "If they think of landing troops, let them go ahead." He said Cubans would defend their country no matter what, and he ended his speech outside the cemetery with the defiant words "*¡Patria o Muerte!*"— "Fatherland or Death!"[6]

As the revolutionary government took shape, Eloy grew to realize he had many differences with the *fidelistas*. It bothered him that Castro appeared to be accumulating more and more power, and that the government had begun to receive high-level delegations from the Soviet Union. It also became clear to Eloy that he would not be offered any meaningful post in the new government. Although there was talk about making him ambassador to China, he suspected Castro might be trying to send him as far away as possible.

Late one night in Havana, Eloy and one of his officers, Captain Roger Redondo, had arrived at the Chinese restaurant El Pekín for dinner when a leading member of Castro's 26th of July Movement, Augusto Martínez Sánchez, appeared at the door. Augusto told Eloy he had just come out of a high-level meeting, and what they discussed was so important that Raúl Castro probably would want to fill him in right away.

Augusto made a call on his military radio, and in less than ten minutes Fidel's brother arrived at the restaurant with a few cars filled with soldiers, who walked in with him. Raúl had recently been named head of the armed forces. Like Eloy, he also had led a rebel battalion called the Second Front. But while Fidel sanctioned his brother's Second Front, he granted no such honor to Eloy.

Leaders of the revolution walk arm-in-arm at the head of a funeral procession for victims of the *La Coubre* explosion on March 5, 1960. From left to right are Fidel Castro; the first president of post-Batista Cuba, Osvaldo Dórtico; Ernesto "Che" Guevara; Augusto Martínez Sánchez; Antonio Nuñez Jimenez; William Morgan; and Eloy Gutiérrez Menoyo. (AP/Wide World Photos)

Raúl greeted Eloy warmly, and the two sat down along with Roger and Augusto. Roger recalled Raúl's words.

"What we have to do is something that we don't want to do, but there is no other alternative," Raúl began, facing Eloy across the table. He said the variety of groups that joined forces against Batista posed a potential threat to the revolution because the Americans would certainly try to exploit any divisions among them.

If given the chance, he continued, "the Americans will overthrow the government. So, we've decided to form a group—a single party—that will be called *Organizaciones Revolucionarias Integradas* and will bring together the 26th of July Movement, the Revolutionary Directorate, the Second National Front of the Escambray, and the Popular Socialist Party."

The conversation stretched on, with Raúl calmly explaining why one party was the only way. Eloy wasn't convinced, though, and tension grew in their voices.

"That isn't what we fought for, what the men died for in the war," Eloy argued. "We fought for democracy, for more parties, a plurality of parties, a free press and all of that. And if a single party is formed, I won't participate."

Raúl insisted there was no choice and that unity was the best way to confront attempts at meddling by the U.S. government, which had backed a coup in Guatemala in 1954 and was similarly trying to exercise control in countries all across Latin America.

"The American government won't accept it if we have a democratic revolution. It's the same as Guatemala," Raúl said. "They bring money, and they begin to give money to the parties."

Eloy heard Raúl out, then repeated his refusal to join the new party.

"What I can do is tell the men of the Second Front that those who want to join the party can do it. But I can't accept that. I'm going to propose dissolving the Second Front of the Escambray. Let it be dissolved. And those who want to go on their own or accept that, then let them do it. But I won't."

Dawn was near when they ended their conversation in profound disagreement. Later that day, Eloy called a meeting to dissolve the Second National Front of the Escambray. Some allied themselves with the government. Others sided with Eloy.

At her wedding on November 5, 1960, Nancy Espinosa Vergara walked down the church aisle in a white dress and promised to spend the rest of her life with Benjamín Lledes Aguila, a twenty-nine-year-old foundry worker who made replacement parts for the nearby sugar mill.

Like Nancy, Benjamín had backed the revolution in secret, selling rebel bonds and sometimes setting fire to cane fields in acts of sabotage. He fervently supported the revolutionary changes being instituted by the new government.

By the time Nancy and Benjamín were married, relations between Cuba and the United States had turned openly hostile. When U.S. oil companies with refineries on the island refused to accept Soviet oil, Cuba nationalized the refineries, and President Dwight Eisenhower retaliated by drastically cutting Cuban sugar imports. Cuba then seized more American properties, including utilities, banks, and sugar mills, and the U.S. government instituted an economic embargo outlawing most trade with the island.[7]

Among the companies nationalized was Benjamín's employer, the MacFarlane Foundry, a complex of workshops along the railroad tracks previously owned by an American. Before the revolution, employees at the foundry had earned as little as half a peso a day. But from then on, they earned a full peso every day.

Once Eloy split with the revolutionary government, he knew his days on the island were numbered. When two of his lieutenants were arrested as counterrevolutionaries, he began to worry he might be next. On the night of January 26, 1961, Eloy and more than a dozen dissidents, among them men who had belonged to the Second Front, boarded two small boats and set out across the ninety-mile passage to Florida. That same month, the U.S. government severed diplomatic ties with Cuba.

Upon their arrival in Key West, Eloy and his men requested political asylum and were taken to an immigration detention center in McAllen, Texas. Once there, they were told about a camp in Guatemala where the CIA was training a force of exiles to invade Cuba. A few Pentagon officials visited to ask Eloy if he and the others would like to join, but he was sure those involved in the plot were *batistianos* more interested in regaining their old positions and properties than in restoring democracy. Eloy was convinced most Cubans would side with Castro rather than with a band of rebels supported by the Americans. So he turned down the invitation to join the invasion force. "It will be eaten up in seventy-two hours," he warned them.

Secret plans for an attack on Cuba had already been approved at the highest levels of the U.S. government when John F. Kennedy was elected president in November 1960. He was briefed by the CIA on the training it was providing to a brigade of anti-Castro Cubans, and he reluctantly gave the go-ahead for the operation.[8] To clear the way for the invasion force, B-26 bombers piloted by Americans and Cuban exiles swooped over Cuban air bases dropping bombs in April 1961. The intent was to knock out much of the Cuban air force, but the attacks also killed seven people and wounded dozens in Havana. At a funeral for the victims, Castro lashed out at the United States, comparing the attack to Pearl Harbor.[9]

"What the imperialists haven't been able to forgive us is that we are here and we have made a socialist revolution under the very noses of the United States," he said. It was the first time Castro publicly declared his revolution to be socialist.[10]

Within hours, ships carrying the invasion force neared the Bahía de Cochinos, or Bay of Pigs. Its members called themselves Brigade 2506, after the serial number of a volunteer who had died during training in Guatemala.[11] The operation's planners had chosen one of Cuba's most sparsely populated areas, the remote beaches and rocky shorelines fringing the Zapata Swamp, which stretched across more than 500,000 acres of forests and marshes. Along the coast, armies of land crabs scurried through thick brush bristling with thorns sharp enough to tear clothing.

An advance landing party in a raft hit a coral reef that dark night off Playa Girón. Most of the men had slipped over the side to head for shore when a jeep appeared on the beach. Its headlights turned toward them, and in an instant a CIA frogman who had his rifle pointed over the bow opened fire. He and the others in the party riddled the jeep with bullets, killing two militiamen who had been on patrol.[12]

As the first of nearly 1,500 Cuban exiles came ashore about 1 a.m. on April 17, militiamen and civilians who survived the firefights fled and quickly passed along word of the attack to the authorities.

Benjamín had been called up for militia duty in Matanzas following the air raids two days earlier. His wife, desperately worried for his safety, had cried as he left.

In the early morning darkness, Benjamín's militia company was awakened and ordered to leave immediately for Playa Girón. The newly trained militiamen snatched up assault rifles, machine guns, and ammunition before heading south in a convoy of trucks.

When they reached the town of Jagüey Grande on the edge of the Zapata Swamp, people in the streets shouted to them, "Watch out! They've been bombing over there." Undeterred, they continued down the road toward Playa Larga in the early morning light, then stepped off the trucks to continue on foot toward an area where paratroopers had been seen floating down from planes.

Some of the militiamen were sent to hunt down the paratroopers, while the rest marched cautiously on. When they heard warplanes approaching, Benjamín and the others hid along the side of the road. But when they spotted the white star of the Cuban air force on one plane, they eagerly stepped out and waved. Benjamín spotted a gunner at the tail of the plane with a .50 caliber machine gun. The plane turned, headed toward them, and began firing. Benjamín had no time to think. As rockets exploded nearby and bullets ricocheted off the road, he hurled himself into a ditch. Four of his comrades were killed.

The militiamen moved on to other areas, firing off mortars whenever they neared enemy positions. The fighting lasted through the day and long into the night. Shells exploded nearby, the air stank of gunpowder, and tanks rolled down the road. When the gunfire halted and the invaders appeared to be retreating, Benjamín and his company eventually returned to the Central Australia sugar mill on the north side of the swamp. With the only telephone in the area, the mill had been set up as their combat headquarters.

On the morning of April 19, Benjamín and others in his company were drinking coffee, groggy from a broken sleep on the hard ground, when two planes roared overhead. As bullets tore into a brick wall nearby, Benjamín threw himself toward a tree to take cover. He was terrified, and as one of the other men landed on top of him, Benjamín felt a sharp blow to the back of his head. In that instant, he thought he had met his end, but it turned out to be a collision with his comrade's rifle butt.

As he regained his senses, he heard antiaircraft guns firing back. Then he saw one of the enemy planes go down in the distance, billowing smoke.

Early the next morning, Castro declared victory over the invading "mercenaries." Although some managed to escape by ship, 1,189 men from the invasion force were taken prisoner and more than one hundred of them were killed in the battle.[13]

In Havana, Paquito's mother woke him.

"What is it?" he asked sleepily.

"It's over. They caught everyone at Girón," she said. "And we lost."

Back in Sagua la Grande, Nancy heard a rumor that Benjamín had been

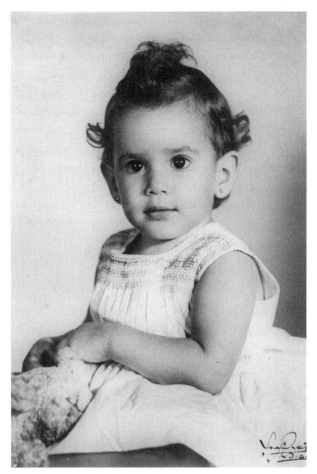

Nancy, circa 1963. (Courtesy of the Lledes family)

killed. She rushed to Matanzas in dread, but when she arrived was thrilled to learn he was not among the more than 150 "martyrs" killed at Playa Girón. Benjamín soon returned home in a truck and trudged to his front door, his pack slung over his shoulder. He embraced his wife and greeted his neighbors, who eagerly questioned him about the battle. He was somber as he remembered comrades who died and recounted how his company had helped defeat the *yanquis*. He returned to work at the foundry, and nearly one year later his daughter was born. Named Nancy after her mother, the little girl took her first steps in a country once again at peace.

Months after the Bay of Pigs invasion, Eloy Gutiérrez Menoyo was released from the immigration jail in Texas. He headed straight to Miami, planning to begin his own fight against Castro. There he met his sweetheart, Tania Sala, who had left Cuba soon after he fled. She was sixteen and he was twenty-six, and by the end of the year they were married. Tania knew from the start that, for Eloy, his family often would have to take second place to his politics. Years later, she told her daughter that she always knew her husband was a patriot whose convictions required his total commitment to the cause.

In the evenings, Eloy held secret meetings at his home in Miami to discuss strategy with Cuban exiles who shared his views. Together they founded a paramilitary group called Alpha 66 and began to gather money and arms. With assault rifles and several small boats, they carried out clandestine attacks off the Cuban coast, raiding military camps and firing on merchant ships doing business with Cuba.

Eloy and about thirty members of the group set up a secret camp on Williams Island, a small, uninhabited cay in the southern Bahamas where their only companions seemed to be reef fish, seabirds, and the occasional shark. The men hid their small boats along the island's coast in canals lined with mangrove trees. They made camp at an abandoned sponge processing plant with a long, stone-lined pool that had been used for washing sponges. When it rained, water rushed in sheets from the roof through aluminum gutters, filling the pool with clear drinking water and making their existence on the island possible.

Small groups of Eloy's men regularly traveled by boat to the Cuban coast, where they scouted out defenses and from time to time started gunfights at military outposts. Some of Eloy's men once wounded several Russian soldiers in an attack on a Soviet military camp. During the raid, they noticed the Soviets were building missile launch pads on the north-central coast. They had no way of knowing the launch pads were intended for nuclear weapons—or that those missiles would lead the world to the brink of nuclear war in October of 1962.

Soon after, they heard the news on their portable radio that the missile crisis had ended with the Soviets' agreement to withdraw their missiles in exchange for an American pledge not to invade Cuba.

While the rest of the world could now afford to forget about Cuba, the island remained a constant obsession for Eloy and his men. At night, near their smoldering cooking fire, they lay in their hammocks with cigarettes glowing in the dark, talking about the battles they had waged and the fights that lay ahead. From their island base, they plotted a new war to set the revolution back on course.

A Musical Boy, a Beach Idyll, a Rebel Plot

Tito Rivera was a strict father to whom music was everything. He ran his business from a cramped one-room office filled with clarinets, flutes, saxophones, strings, reeds, printed music, a wooden desk, and an old phonograph. Tito had played tenor saxophone in the army band, and in military style he wrote out Paquito's schedule on a chalkboard each day—from making the beds in the morning to leaving for rehearsals in the afternoon. He would not tolerate mischief, and he sometimes used his belt to whip Paquito when he misbehaved.

Paquito studied clarinet after school at the Alejandro García Caturla Municipal Conservatory, a single-story building in Marianao with a marble bust of José Martí near the entrance.

Tito regularly stopped by the school to check on his son. One afternoon, he couldn't find Paquito anywhere. He searched inside and out, and then looked up and saw him clinging to the branches of a tree outside the school. Paquito was surprised to see his father, and his father was furious to see him clowning around instead of rehearsing.

"Now you'll see," he threatened. "I'm going to punish you. You won't be allowed out of the house."

Paquito didn't answer and climbed down without saying a word. Lolita Torres, a teacher who was there that day and who was fond of Paquito, urged Tito to go easy. "Don't scold him," she implored.

"It's your fault as teachers that Paquito is acting like this," Tito replied curtly. And as he turned to leave, he told his son, "We'll deal with this at home."

Later that day at school, Lolita asked Paquito, "Why do you do that to your father?"

"I don't mean anything bad by it," he said. "It's that I really want to play."

Paquito and his younger brother Enrique relished escaping from their father's regime of music study whenever possible. Often they left the house together and went four doors down the street to the neighborhood movie theater, Cine Cándido.

For the ten-cent admission, the boys watched Bugs Bunny and other cartoons and American movies with subtitles. Paquito didn't just enjoy the movies; he also relished making mischief in the theater.

One day, sitting in the balcony with Enrique, Paquito delightedly tossed talcum powder over the edge, which fell on the first-floor audience like snow.

Another day, in the front row this time, the two boys were so close to the screen that there was little room for a cat to get by as it slunk past at their feet. Paquito pounced and swiftly grabbed the cat. It was a quiet moment in the movie, and Paquito threw the cat toward the screen. "MRYAAAAAAAAAAAWR!" The cat's cry echoed through the theater. The cat dug its claws into the screen and hung there for a moment, then fell back, hit the ground, and raced off.

The audience went right back to watching the movie, but it wasn't long before a theater employee came to the snickering brothers and escorted them out. "After that day, they didn't let us in anymore," Enrique recalled years later with a grin.

Twice a week, Paquito went to study at the home of his music teacher, the respected conductor and composer Félix Guerrero.

Maestro Guerrero taught Paquito music theory, harmony, counterpoint, and composition. When he was only six, Paquito had played the saxophone in one of the composer's concerts. Several years later, Maestro Guerrero felt the boy was ready to advance to a level that few students ever reach.

Sitting at the piano, he told Paquito, "Music is a language, the language of sound. In school, you have your subjects that help you master it. But what your mind, your heart, tells you when you compose is very impor-

Paquito playing with toy guns along with his friend Dinorah, late 1950s.
(Courtesy of Dinorah Valdés Pérez)

Paquito after Castro's rise to power, circa 1960. (Courtesy of
Paquito D'Rivera)

tant. The rest is extra, extra technical skills that will help you express yourself strongly and make sure that what you want to say comes out right."

Paquito listened, then replied, "I'm going to do it."

In the years that followed, some would listen to Paquito's music and
say he had indeed created his own language.

Eloy's secret missions often kept him away from his wife and newborn
daughter, Elena Patricia. While Tania stayed with the baby in Miami, Eloy
was off with his men in the Bahamas and the Dominican Republic. He
wrote Tania frequent letters, saying in one, "Unfortunately this fight is
hard and requires all kinds of actions in emotional times, which without
a doubt strengthen the struggle and awaken those who are asleep."

Some Cuban exiles suspiciously questioned where Eloy's loyalties lay. Less than two years before he fled Cuba, he had defended Fidel Castro against a plot to overthrow his government. After Eloy left, some Cubans surmised he had been plotting against Castro from the beginning and had begun cooperating to foil the plot only after learning that the government suspected him of being a traitor.

Eloy said that there was nothing to such theories and that his intentions were pure. He told Fidel about the plot before it began to unfold, and they agreed Eloy would play along to lay a trap for the conspirators. Eloy and one of his commanders from the Second Front, an American named William Morgan, soon won the confidence of the plotters, who included Batista supporters in Miami and Havana as well as one of Fidel's fiercest opponents, the Dominican dictator Rafael Trujillo. Eloy later revealed that William first received word of the plan from an American who had links to the Mafia and had offered one million dollars for Castro's assassination.

Eloy acted the part of a counterrevolutionary for about six months in 1959, helping pick up weapons shipments parachuted into Cuba and maintaining contact with conspirators in Miami, Havana, and Santo Domingo. By August, Castro decided to end the charade. Eloy and his men captured conspirators at gunpoint at three houses in Havana, turning over more than one hundred of them to the authorities.[1]

Within days, Eloy helped lure a plane to Cuba with an arms shipment by sending a radio message that rebels had taken the city of Trinidad on the edge of the Sierra del Escambray. A priest sent by Trujillo came onto the flight and promised to send another plane the next night with more weapons and reinforcements. Castro oversaw the operation from a mango orchard alongside the airstrip.[2]

The next day, heavily armed Cuban soldiers were in positions around the airfield when the second plane touched down with ten men on board. Outside on the runway, a group of men posing as conspirators approached the parked plane. When they told the crew they were under arrest, gunfire erupted.[3] Two on board were killed, along with two on the ground. The rest of the crew surrendered, and the plane lay abandoned on the runway, riddled with bullet holes.[4]

Eloy's smiling face appeared in Cuban magazines as the hero who had defended the revolution by pretending to oppose it.

After he left the island for Miami, though, Eloy became a target for

harsh criticism. Che Guevara called him and his men *comevacas*—cow eat-
ers, or cattle rustlers—saying they had simply taken the cows of peasants
while doing no real fighting during the war.[5] Fidel said Eloy's group Alpha
66 was closely allied with the CIA, while Eloy denied any personal link to
the Americans.

It was true that the CIA had tried to recruit a number of his friends.
From time to time, one would tell Eloy the CIA had made contact and
offered a course in telegraphy or some other subject. Take it, Eloy would
advise them. Once their courses were over, Eloy said, his friends generally
dropped their contact with the agency.

The CIA was trying to recruit many exiles in Miami who shared the
common goal of overthrowing Castro. But Eloy and his closest supporters
said they preferred an independent route, and they worked to raise money
for their struggle through fundraising letters, benefit events, and even
some boxing matches.

In one open letter focused on fundraising, Eloy described "Plan
Omega," a new strategy to topple Castro's government. "It is a Cuban
plan started with Cuban resources but one that needs the moral and
financial support of those free men who love freedom and democracy, and
who understand the need for an effective fight against communism. We
will fight in Cuba to destroy it." He signed the letter beneath the slogan
"VICTORY OR DEATH."

Before dawn on December 28, 1964, Eloy and three of his men stepped
out of a twenty-five-foot boat and stood on a white sand beach near the
lighthouse of Punta Caleta in eastern Cuba. The four unloaded their pro-
visions and hid in the trees and brush along the shore. Another man, who
had brought them, left with the boat and headed back for their camp in
the Dominican Republic. Their mission was so secret that even Eloy's wife
didn't know where he was. The rebels hoped to start an insurrection, but
in the next few weeks, they found little support among the peasants and
instead found themselves on the run, followed by a helicopter and shot at
by militiamen pursuing them mercilessly through the hills.

When their rations ran out, they turned to picking guavas and bananas,
and filled their canteens with rainwater from puddles. Sometimes they
ordered people they encountered to prepare food for them. For weeks, the
four managed to evade their pursuers. But on January 23, 1965, less than

a month after their arrival, they awoke to find their camp surrounded by militiamen. They surrendered and were flown by helicopter to Santiago, where Eloy was separated from the other three.

His captors blindfolded him. He was certain he would be executed before a firing squad—the sentence that corresponded to his crime. Instead, his captors took him away in a car and then transferred him to a plane.

When the plane landed, Eloy had no idea where he was. He was led indoors. Someone removed the blindfold. Across a table sat Fidel Castro. Raúl stood nearby. Top officers stood along the walls. Even decades later, Eloy remembered Fidel's words clearly.

"I knew you were coming, and we caught you—alive or dead—but we caught you, because when you say something, you mean it. You said you were coming. I knew you were coming. But now you know we're going to execute you, don't you?"

"Yes," Eloy said. "But will you let me clear up one thing?"

Eloy started by contrasting his childhood under a dictatorship in Spain to the freedom he found in Cuba.

"I learned what a free country was like, a country where my parents didn't have to tell me what I should say and shouldn't say. . . . When I arrived, there was liberty, and I found a free country. Then out of the blue came the coup by Batista. I continued fighting. . . . And later on as a rebel, I continued on and on. Now, you tell me you're going to kill me. I don't have anything against you. I hold no resentment whatsoever. You're going to kill me. So kill me."

"But wouldn't you like to save your life?"

"No. Because I'd have to pay a very high price," Eloy said.

"You don't have to pay a high price," Fidel said. "You don't want to hear my terms? . . . However you get through this, those who came with you will, too."

"No, each one of us decides for himself," Eloy countered.

"No," Fidel said. "If you save your life, all of their lives will be saved. If you don't save your life, no one's will be saved. Look, one of the terms is that you be willing to go on television and say the *campesinos* were hostile toward you."

Eloy decided it wouldn't be a lie to say some of those he encountered were hostile, though he wouldn't mention those who were friendly. Fidel also asked him to answer whether other Cuban exiles were planning similar raids. Eloy said no. He thought if others landed in Cuba, they wouldn't come independently; they would have American support. He agreed to Fidel's terms and appeared on television.

The special program on February 2, 1965, was hosted by the well-known announcer Manolo Ortega, who began: "Dear viewers, today our cameras and microphones will bring you an interview whose transcendence cannot be denied. Appearing before you is the counterrevolutionary ringleader Eloy Gutiérrez Menoyo, who as is known came ashore with three followers near Baracoa and was recently captured by forces of the mountain militias and the 50th Division of the Army of Oriente."[6]

The host introduced two state security agents who would be questioning Eloy and the other three prisoners.

"Menoyo, on what date did you arrive in the United States?"

"December of 1960 or January of 1961."

"When you arrived, what did you do?"

"We were arrested by the American authorities when we got there and were kept in a camp in Texas for four and a half months."

"What did they ask you?"

"They asked us about current economic, political, and military information at that time in Cuba."

"And what information did you give?"

"What I had knowledge of at that time."

Eloy explained how after he was released he began to reorganize the Second Front and raise money to buy boats and arms. Asked why they needed the weapons, Eloy said it was "to begin operations against merchant ships and against different targets."

The interrogator pressed the point. "You talked about how you attacked, you carried out pirate attacks against a Russian ship and an English ship among other crimes you committed. Were those ships armed with artillery?"

"No, they didn't have artillery, they were merchant ships," Eloy said.

One of the agents turned his questioning to Eloy's comrade Ramón Quesada, asking if the men had received some type of training to carry out their attacks.

"Well, I was working for a time in the Central Intelligence Agency, and there they taught me how to handle explosives, and photographs of maps, how to take apart some types of weapons that I wasn't familiar with, like a .30 caliber and other things," Ramón replied.

"What other groups of counterrevolutionaries that you know of have carried out that kind of action?"

"Well, the *Comandos Mambises*, and other people who worked for the CIA," Ramón explained.

The questioning went on, with Eloy answering that yes, it was true his force had the same aims as the Americans. But he also said that he had a very low opinion of Manuel Artime, one of the leaders of the Bay of Pigs invasion. Eloy said he thought Artime was capable of launching another attack on Cuba only if he were accompanied by the U.S. Navy, but not if his troops were alone.

"What opinion do you have of the counterrevolutionary organizations outside the country?"

"Very bad, they have very low morale," Eloy replied honestly.

"What are the counterrevolutionary organizations that you headed?"

"The Revolutionary Movement of the People, the Second Front, and Alpha 66."

Eloy explained how his men once had a camp in the Bahamas, then later moved to the Dominican Republic. They had set up their base at Punta Presidente near the border with Haiti, where Eloy said a colonel in the Dominican military brought them 400 grenades and 15,000 rounds of ammunition.

"What plans did you have with those men?"

"To begin to infiltrate little by little in small groups."

"With what goal?"

"Overthrowing the government."

The agent asked Eloy what he found upon his arrival.

"Well, I found the *campesinos* in a completely hostile situation," Eloy said.

"Did the people join you?"

"No, not at all."

The show was wrapping up. One of the interrogators asked, "Menoyo, what experience have you come away with? . . . What conclusion have you drawn from this?"

Eloy answered that he had previously thought most people in Cuba were against the communist system and ready to take up arms. But once he and his men landed, they found many *campesinos* quickly reported them to the army, and that kept them on the run.

"After what's been said, the only thing left for me to do is warn my comrades and my friends to think hard about things," Eloy said. "You could have worse luck than we did."

"One last question," the agent said. He asked whether Eloy thought it was possible to effectively fight against the will of the Cuban people.

"Against the people, I think, one definitely cannot fight."

"Do you think what you did was right, or was your cause unjust?"

Eloy replied with a carefully worded answer: If all of the Cuban people support the current government, he said, such actions are "totally unjust."

"What did you say?"

"If all of the people support this, it's unjust to fight."

"And you doubt that the people support this?"

"What I saw, at least, is that the people are with this."

The announcer said the questioning was finished, adding that it had shown "the enormous and crushing strength of the revolution, and the weakness and moral ruin of the counterrevolution."

"Events tell us every day that there is nothing and no one who can halt the march of our glorious revolution. Events tell us how, in every corner of the country, the Rebel Army, the militias, the Department of State Security, and all of the people as they work and build the new socialist society are on alert and vigilant, and willing to sweep away CIA agents and traitors of all sorts who try to infiltrate to carry out criminal plans ordered by their imperialist masters."

"Thank you very much for your attention," the announcer said, "and good night."[7]

Eloy later insisted he and his men had come independently, but they were swiftly convicted of counterrevolutionary crimes as "agents of a foreign power." Eloy was sentenced to thirty years in prison.

On the surface, life remained peaceful in Nancy's small town of Sagua la Grande, where pedestrians strolled down wide thoroughfares named after long-dead patriots—Céspedes, Martí, and Gómez. Royal palms and *flamboyán* trees stood along the slow-flowing river in the heart of town. Sagua la Grande had been built on trade through the nearby port of Isabela de Sagua and on sugar, processed under the smokestack on the edge of town.

But changes were coming to the area that directly affected many people. When the family of one-year-old Nancy moved to a new home, the government had more of a role in that process than it would have had just years earlier. A second-story apartment had been abandoned by a wealthy family who opposed the revolution and had left the country. The government promptly assigned the apartment to Nancy's parents, who moved out of their small wooden house and joined the toddler's grandparents, uncle, and aunt in their spacious new home. They bought the gas stove they found there from the government, along with a couple of rocking chairs and a sofa that the prior owners had left behind. The government sold off the rest of the furniture, and the new tenants began paying rent to the state.

In the eyes of the authorities, the pharmacist who had moved out of the apartment and abandoned the country had forfeited his right to the property. He also left behind his pharmacy on the first floor of the building. That, too, belonged to the state now.

Havana had a long tradition of jazz, of infectious grooves descended from *danzón* improvisations and New Orleans–style Dixieland that floated out of clubs and hotels into the night air. Paquito grew up hearing the sounds of trumpets, saxophones, and clarinets mixed with the distinctly Cuban percussion of the *clave*, *tumbadora*, *batá*, and *bongó*. But the swing and improvisation of American jazz interested him more. As a teenager he was thrilled to go along whenever musicians got together for what they called a *descarga*—an unloading, a letting loose. In short, a jam session.

Once, when Paquito was in his early teens, a friend tried to talk Paquito's father into letting him join a jam session at the Cabaret Parisien in the Hotel Nacional.

"I'll take care of him," promised Alberto Romeu, a young drummer.

Tito resisted, but it helped that Alberto was the son of the director of the navy band, whom Tito knew from his days in the army band.

"All right," Tito said, "I'll trust you because you're the son of Captain Romeu."

As the two left, Tito warned Alberto, "Bring him back early."

Paquito took his saxophone to the cabaret and joined in the jam session. Although he was already famous as a child soloist, most of his training had been in classical music. The chance to improvise made the evening special for Paquito, and when Alberto suggested it was time to leave, he resisted.

"You can't stay. You have to go and I have to take you back home," Alberto said.

Paquito pouted as they left in a taxi.

"I hate my father," he told Alberto. "My father doesn't let me live."

"Hey, Paquito, what your father has done for you is a big favor. Look how you can play. And you've got to thank your father for that. Someday in your life, you're going to realize what he's done for you."

In his daily life, Paquito didn't concern himself with the societal changes underway in Cuba, but his parents resented the growing demands the communist system placed on their lives. Adults were expected to belong to the neighborhood "Committees for the Defense of the Revolution," which held regular meetings to discuss Castro's speeches or issues facing the nation. The committees also arranged neighborhood patrols to report any suspicious activities, and members now had the power to accuse neighbors of being subversives or counterrevolutionaries. The government declared military service to be mandatory, and young men could be called to three years of service starting at age sixteen.

Paquito's parents felt the military service requirement interfered with their son's future. When his call-up notice came in 1965, shortly before his seventeenth birthday, he was regularly performing at the Musical Theater of Havana. Paquito's mother was horrified at the thought of her son possibly having to go to battle, and talk of being prepared for another American invasion was rampant. Maura wasn't a pacifist. She was proud that her father had fought in the War of Independence against Spain and had won a medal. But now, she felt there was nothing worth defending.

All she knew was that Paquito had to be dropped off early on the specified date at the baseball park known as La Tropical. That morning, Tito told his son he wouldn't be accompanying him to the ballpark. Paquito and his mother got into the family's 1941 Plymouth and were on their way when they realized they had forgotten something at home and turned back.

Opening the door, Paquito found his father slumped in a chair, still in his pajamas, weeping. It was the only time Paquito could remember seeing his father cry.

It was no easier for his mother at the stadium. Hundreds of young men stood on the baseball field with their families, waiting to depart. Maura had no idea where Paquito would be taken. She felt as if the government could do anything it wanted with him.

Paquito joined the other recruits as they were ordered to climb into waiting trucks. As the truck that carried Paquito pulled away, Maura ran after it.

She kept running, tears streaming down her face, until a woman stopped her. The stranger took hold of her and said, "¿Estás loca? Calm down. Wait."

Soon after his sentencing, Eloy was locked up alone in a hospital ward at Havana's main State Security building. There were ten beds, and all except his lay empty. A guard was posted outside the barred door, but Eloy began to imagine escape when he noticed two high windows on a wall that the guard couldn't see from his post.

During the night, after Eloy had been faking sleep for some time, he slipped out of bed, leaving his sheets and pillow in a bundle that he was confident would fool the guard in the darkness. Eloy moved silently toward the wall, clutching a three-inch-long flat piece of metal that he had broken off from the drawer of his bedside table.

Trying not to make a sound, he opened the window and climbed into the space between the window and the bars that were flush with the outer wall. Through the bars, Eloy could see another wall that ran along the edge of a lighted parking lot. He thought if he could use the piece of metal to file down the corner of the wall where it met the bars, he could slip through and escape along the outer wall, then climb down an electrical pole next to it. With any luck, he could make it to the street and disappear into the city.

Grasping the piece of metal, he began to file away at the wall next to the bars. He thought it must have been midnight already, because there was no movement in the parking lot. After about an hour of work, Eloy closed the window as he climbed back down and slipped into bed. The guard, still sitting outside holding his gun, hadn't noticed.

The next night, Eloy asked the guard to turn off the light so he could sleep better. From his bed in the darkened room, he could see the guard sitting a dozen feet away in the lighted entryway. As soon as Eloy thought it safe, he made his move back to the window, again leaving behind the pile of sheets and pillow. In the parking lot below, Eloy occasionally saw an agent walk to his car and pull away. No one noticed Eloy's work. He shaved away at the concrete-like wall with his file, gradually opening a space.

It was painstaking work. On his tenth night, Eloy could almost slip through. He thought it would take a tiny bit more filing and the opening would be wide enough.

Just as he was finishing for the night and about to step back down into the room, a guard's face suddenly appeared through the window. The guard had hoisted himself up on the outside simply to call out and startle the guard on duty inside. But he and Eloy came face-to-face, and both were shocked.

The response was immediate. Lights were flicked on, and guards rushed in. They grabbed Eloy, led him away to a cell, and locked the door. Eloy cursed to himself. It would not be his last attempt to escape.

The first few months of Eloy's imprisonment were the most difficult. His mind flitted from his predicament to the outside life he could no longer experience—his wife, daughter, freedom. But he realized some thoughts could torture him. If he wanted to survive, he would have to readapt his mind so as not to let in too much. Tune out memories that could be destructive, he told himself. Forget the outside world, forget everything.

Each year, Nancy looked forward to finishing the school term in July and beginning her vacation. She and her family packed up enough clothes, food, and supplies to last for weeks, and they got on a bus bound for the coast. At the last stop, they stepped off and joined others on a truck that made trips along the bumpy dirt road to Uvero, a seaside village of simple wooden cabins.

Nancy loved the freshness of the sea air that blew across the coastal mangroves; she described it as divine. Uvero's cabins were built on stilts directly over the water. A series of wooden piers linked the homes to the shore and to each other. The family's cabin had belonged to Nancy's grandfather since it was built in the 1940s. From the front deck she enjoyed watching the waves gently rolling in from the Atlantic.

Inside the cabin, she lay listening to the sound of water lapping against wood, and looked up at the ceiling, running her eyes along the fan-shaped palm fronds bound together in the thatched roof. When the wind was strong, she heard the waves splashing against the wood below her. The water was shallow, and the houses stood on a sea bottom of large-grained sand, mud, and bits of mangrove roots.

Sometimes Nancy and the other children dangled fishing lines out the window. When they caught a fish, they pulled it up, watched it flapping as it hit the wood, and killed it out of curiosity, not thinking of cooking or eating it.

Nancy with her parents and another boy at Uvero, mid-1960s. (Courtesy of the Lledes family)

Nancy's grandfather, who was a serious fisherman, admonished the children, "Why do you kill it if you aren't going to eat it?" He caught his own bait by wading in and casting his net, then dumping the minnows he gathered into a bucket filled with seawater. Nancy and her sister and brother followed their grandfather out onto the pier at night to fish, struggling to keep up with his long steps. Carrying spools of fishing line, they baited their hooks with their grandfather's bait. Then they let their weighted hooks drop into water as black as the night sky.

Nancy's grandfather was a mathematics teacher, and he was known for throwing erasers at pupils who didn't pay attention, so his grandchildren listened when he told them to stay quiet. He said talking would scare away the fish. The children held their fishing lines in silence, or whispered to each other when they could no longer contain themselves.

Sometimes they brought up their hooks with *pargo* and *caballerote*, types of snapper with silvery reddish skin, and the family cooked them over coals. Neighbors often came to visit, and Nancy's aunt played the accordion. There was no electricity, so at night they lit kerosene lamps.

The tranquility of Uvero seeped inside Nancy, and it would never leave her.

At that same time, Eloy was being held at the Model Prison on Isla de Pinos, the largest penitentiary in Cuba. The prison was near the island's north shore and was made up of five circular buildings that resembled coliseums, four of them filled with thousands of prisoners in cells that circled the buildings' giant inner chambers. Each circular, as they were called, had five levels of cells and a concrete tower in the inner chamber where guards kept watch over the prisoners. From some spots on the higher floors, the inmates could see the Caribbean in the distance.

Rats scurried through the halls, and the inmates' meals of vegetable broth or macaroni were meager and bland. Eloy recalled frequent beatings of prisoners by the guards, who sometimes even used bayonets to prick or slap inmates.

All prisoners were expected to work, and Eloy was assigned to a crew that went by truck each morning to a quarry to extract granite and marble. However, considering himself a political prisoner and a prisoner of war, he began to refuse to go when the guards came calling. Eloy stayed in his cell as most other prisoners trudged off for work. The men wore straw hats or wetted handkerchiefs on their heads to protect themselves against the blazing heat as they used sledgehammers to split granite boulders that had been blasted loose from a rock face.

For weeks, the guards had been telling Eloy he had to join the other inmates and work. He told the guards they could do whatever they wished but that there was no way they could make him go along. One morning after most in the circular had left for the quarry, Eloy was in his cell when he heard a guard call out his name, ordering him to report to the first floor. Eloy had just stepped through the cell's open door into the hallway when guards ambushed him. Shoving him and hitting him, they forced him into a jeep for the trip to the quarry. On the way, one held him in a headlock while several others pummeled him. A second group followed behind in another jeep.

Once they arrived at the quarry, three guards pulled him out of the vehicle. He tried to resist, but a barrage of fists tore at his body while other guards yelled insults at him. A fourth officer joined in, whipping Eloy with the flat side of his machete. As the guards cursed and shoved him, Eloy staggered toward a nearby carpentry shop.

Another prisoner, Fernando Pruna, was at the shop replacing the splintered handle of his sledgehammer when he heard shouting and looked up to see the guards beating Eloy.

"¡Hijos de putas! Leave him alone!" Fernando shouted. Guards in a watchtower pointed their guns toward Fernando. The blows continued, and Eloy fell to the ground.

Two guards grabbed him by the arms and dragged him back away as a truck quickly approached and stopped next to them. Fernando watched as four guards grabbed Eloy by the arms and legs and heaved him onto the bed of the truck. He landed with a thud. The guards got in, and the truck sped off in a cloud of dust.

The world became a blur for Eloy, but he was vaguely aware as he was pushed out of the truck onto the rocky ground. Other prisoners later told him what they saw and heard.

"Are you going to work?" one guard demanded. Eloy, barely conscious, shook his head: No, no, no.

Eloy raised his arms to protect himself as the blows kept falling. He blacked out, then later came to. Bloodied and disoriented, he was led to a truck and driven to the infirmary. The doctor did nothing but tape up his chest so that he could bear the pain of breathing. Many of his ribs were broken, and his face was swollen and bruised.[8] Eloy was in severe pain for weeks, and he never fully recovered. He became deaf in one ear and lost much of the sight in his left eye.

Years later, Eloy told the story of that day very quickly, sparing many of the details as if to avoid reliving the memories.

3

School, Army, Jail

After being captured in a failed rebel assault on Santiago's Moncada barracks in the early days of the revolution in 1953, Fidel Castro famously declared: "Condemn me, it does not matter. History will absolve me." His nationalistic vision of a break with the past appealed to many Cubans. Since the arrival of Columbus, Cuba had been ruled by foreign powers, first under Spain, and later, even after independence, under the strong influence of the United States.

Cuba was long dominated by outsiders who had controlled its sugar and tobacco, and Castro preached forcefully against that past. He cast the revolutionary struggle as a rejection of an old order and the birth of a new, just society. Teaching the poor to read, the government printed textbooks with sentences like "The Revolution wins all its battles," "We won freedom guided by Fidel," "Our people are governed by the people," and "We are united in defense of the Fatherland."

Nationalism, patriotism, and rhetoric proved a powerful mix.

At school in the late 1960s, Nancy and her classmates stood at attention when the teacher entered the room. Together, they repeated a slogan that played upon the double meaning of the word *rajarse*, which means both "to crack" and "to back down."

"Only windows crack. Men die on their feet!" the children repeated.

Other times, the class recited, "With the Fatherland all, without the Fatherland nothing!" or "With Fidel all, without Fidel nothing!"

On Saturdays, Benjamín took the children to the movies. Often they watched Soviet war films dubbed in Spanish.

The battle scenes seemed a world away from the tranquil streets of Sagua la Grande, where people greeted their neighbors while strolling down the sidewalks. At twilight, adults often sat chatting with neighbors by their front doors and on their patios.

Nancy's friends regularly stopped by her house to play after school, but her parents never let the visits get in the way of her studies. Her mother, who was one of six children and had to quit school at seventeen, told her, "I couldn't study because my parents didn't have money to pay for my studies. Now that the state gives you a way to study, you have to keep studying until the end. You have to do what I could never do."

Mornings began with the sounding of a whistle from the foundry at 7 o'clock. Nancy often was eager to get to school early and sometimes became impatient as her mother ironed her uniform—a white blouse and gray skirt.

"*Mami*, I'm going to be late," she repeated anxiously. "I'm going to be late."

Fidel Castro had pledged to turn barracks into classrooms, to make Cuba a country where children could dream and the poor would have work. A literacy campaign was begun in 1961, and soon an estimated 270,000 people were involved in teaching and administering the program.[1] Tens of thousands of students joined volunteer brigades and spread out across the country to teach basic reading and writing. Some members of the brigades wore olive-green uniforms and berets and carried Chinese-made kerosene lamps to teach at night in the countryside. At public events, they sang their own anthem:

We are the Conrado Benítez brigades!
We are the vanguard of the revolution! . . .
Down with imperialism! Up with freedom! . . .
Study, work, rifle! Pencil, handbook, manual!
¡Alfabetizar, alfabetizar, alfabetizar! ¡Venceremos!

Once he became a soldier in the Revolutionary Armed Forces, Paquito was chosen to join the military band, and he moved into the musicians' quarters in the Havana neighborhood of La Víbora. Soon after his arrival, he was eating with other band members when an unfamiliar musician approached their table.

"¡*Qué cara de pato bobo tienes!*" Paquito blurted out. "What a silly duck face you have."

The lanky flutist, Félix Durán, looked at the grinning newcomer with contempt and thought, "This guy and I are going to have problems." He turned and took a seat at another table.

Later, Paquito came up to Félix, grabbed him playfully by the nose, and said, "Isn't that right that you have a nose that looks like a duck's beak?"

Félix was fuming, and Paquito's teasing had only just begun. Later, while Félix was practicing scales in a darkened room during a blackout, Paquito dropped aluminum cooking trays behind him, making him jump. Félix told him in anger several times, "I don't want to be your friend."

But there was something about Paquito that made Félix's anger melt away. Twenty minutes after a prank, Paquito would put an arm around Félix and say, "¡Pato!" So Félix grew used to his new nickname: El Pato.

Paquito's old friend Alberto Romeu was also in the band, and they often played pranks together. One night, the electricity went out while the band director and other officers were holding a meeting in a room at the musicians' quarters. Paquito and Alberto decided to strike in the darkness. They filled two buckets with water and slunk outside to the barred window. On the count of three, they swung the buckets back and let the water fly. They ran, racing two blocks down, then eight or more over. When they thought they were safe, they stopped and leaned over to catch their breath. Then they turned and began to walk back as if nothing had happened. Not a drop of water had fallen on their fatigues.

When Paquito and Alberto came upon a group of officers looking for the culprits, the first angry question was "Where were you?" The sergeants were soaked. The two innocently asked what had happened.

"You know, we were lucky," Alberto later told Paquito.

The band members grew used to Paquito's pranks. He squirted musicians with water guns during rehearsals, and once he hid a crab in a bandmate's baritone saxophone, causing a scandal when—in the middle of the national anthem at a military ceremony—the saxophonist flung the crab into the air and it landed on the neck of a trumpet player.

Another time, Paquito sneaked alongside Félix's bed while he was sleeping and cracked an egg over his face. Paquito said he was making an omelet.

Friends never reported his transgressions. But sometimes when he was caught mouthing off, officers sent him to work in the kitchen, where he peeled potatoes or did whatever else the cook needed.

When the troops went to the countryside to cut sugarcane, Paquito and Félix took spots next to each other and began chopping away with their machetes. The soldiers were supposed to grip the stalks and cut them close to the ground. But paying little attention to technique, Paquito flailed wildly at the cane, cutting the stalks halfway up. His commanding officers concluded he was hopeless in the cane field.

But when he put his hands to the clarinet, his agility and style were unmatched. The band played a wide range of classical music plus the necessary dirges of official funerals. Jazz wasn't part of the repertoire. In fact, some of his superiors saw it as anti-Cuban and a symbol of Yankee imperialism. Paquito recalled in his autobiography *Mi Vida Saxual* (My Sax Life) that once the band director walked in on the musicians in the middle of a jam session. Furious, he told them, "Stop that right now. I don't want to hear one more note. *Compañeros*, jazz represents the enemy."[2]

Eloy had been in prison for nearly two years when his father brought the news he had been expecting: "Your wife, she got a divorce."

Immediately, Eloy felt relieved, as if a burden had been removed. He had sent Tania a message after his capture suggesting they split up. He knew it would be a long sentence and thought divorce would be best. At first, she had resisted, but finally she realized it made sense. He hoped that she would be getting on with her life in Miami at last.

Eloy often thought of the daughter he had left behind with Tania as a two-year-old toddler. He tried to imagine Elena Patricia as a bigger girl, able to do and say so much more.

It was like that with much of his life: he had to imagine it to keep it alive—and yet not concentrate on it. If he did, he felt it would destroy him.

As the years wore on, Eloy was moved from prison to prison throughout the country, from Isla de Pinos, to Guanajay, to La Cabaña, El Príncipe, Boniato, and Combinado del Este.

Each day was the same, so he didn't count them.

"I tried to kill time," Eloy recalled years later, "so that time wouldn't kill me."

He wrote letters to his daughter on thin paper that other prisoners smuggled out during rare visits. At nightfall, as the men lay on their cots, they often played chess. They had no boards, no pieces. So each prisoner carried the game in his head and called out his moves in the darkness.

Eloy held out little hope of being freed, but he stood by his principles. He became known as one of the *plantados*—men planted in the soil like trees. These were the prisoners who refused to give in. Eloy would not accept the so-called rehabilitation plan, in which inmates who acknowledged guilt and pledged allegiance to "revolutionary principles" would receive leniency. More than once, a military officer came to visit Eloy proposing he join the plan, guaranteeing he would be freed within a year if he admitted his mistakes and rejoined the revolution.

"Who's making this offer?" Eloy demanded to know.

"Fidel is," the officer replied.

"Tell Fidel he's the one who should be rehabilitated."

Defiant and determined, Eloy repeatedly led hunger strikes to demand better prison conditions, growing painfully thin. He also refused to put on the blue uniform of a common prisoner, wearing only underwear for years. It remained that way for much of two decades.

Eloy found that one of the best ways to keep occupied was to sing— about love, about freedom, about Cuba. He became a musician of sorts and shared his songs with the other prisoners. He imagined the instruments and tapped out the rhythm against his bed frame or whatever was within reach.

In one protest song, he spoke of climbing to the top of a mountain to join a struggle for Cuba:

> And you will be with me
> Firing off your words
> Until there is light
> In the sky of my country.

In a way, it was only natural for Eloy to be in prison for a political cause. His father, Dr. Carlos Gutiérrez Zavaleta, had been in jail when Eloy was born on December 8, 1934. His father had been serving a sentence for illegally hiding weapons in the family's home in Madrid. As Eloy recalled it, his father had agreed to keep the guns for other socialists who were alarmed by the growing influence of the Spanish right wing. A week after Eloy was born, his mother Mercedes Menoyo Baños carried him to jail to show him to her husband.

Once released from jail, Eloy's father returned to his medical practice, seeing patients at his office across the street from the tree-lined paths and grassy clearings of Madrid's Buen Retiro Gardens. Carlos's office was on the first floor, and the family lived upstairs.

Some of Eloy's first memories were of the bombardments of the Spanish Civil War: the sirens, the trembling of windows in the house, refugees passing in the street. Eloy's family sided with the government and against the insurgents. His sixteen-year-old brother José Antonio was among those who joined the fight, even though he did not tell his family because he was supposedly still too young to enlist in the army.

One day, their mother awoke and leapt from her bed in tears, shouting out that José Antonio had been killed.

Eloy's older brother tried to comfort her, saying it couldn't be true because José Antonio was still in school. "*Mamá*, it was a dream, a nightmare you had."

"No, they've killed him. I saw him in front of my bed, wrapped in his cloak with his neck bleeding."

As it turned out, a bullet had passed through José Antonio's neck during a battle. He had fallen in the snow and died.

Eloy grew up believing his mother's outburst was not a coincidence. His brother had called out to his mother in his final moment, and somehow she had heard him.

When the Spanish Civil War ended and Francisco Franco assumed power, Eloy's father was sent away to Valencia to be tried on suspicion of war crimes. Because he had been a regional health commander for the army under the former government, he was immediately a suspect. Even though he was acquitted, his medical license was rescinded and his career was ruined.

Eloy's mother, meanwhile, had to take care of five children. Food was scarce, and some days she could only give each child a piece of corn bread.

"Keep it and eat it when you can during the day because there is nothing else to eat," she painfully told the children.

To calm their bellies, Eloy and his siblings could get broth with a bit of bread at a charity home where women offered food to needy children.

Eloy's parents eventually decided it was no use staying in Madrid and moved with the family to Barcelona. Eloy earned spare change hailing taxis for passers-by or collecting discarded cigarette butts to resell the remaining tobacco. Sometimes the boys stole garbanzo beans and lentils from merchants' carts by cutting open the sacks and using a bag to catch the stream of beans that flowed out.

When boats filled with tourists arrived at the docks of Barcelona, Eloy dived into the water and called out to passengers for them to throw change. Usually he was able to grasp the glinting coins as they sank. When a cruel tourist would throw a coin especially far, Eloy made the best of it even when he couldn't reach the coin, surfacing in triumph and pretending he had grabbed it.

At the end of World War II, Eloy's parents were disillusioned with life in Spain and decided to move to Cuba, where one of his aunts lived. They settled in Cojímar, a fishing town east of Havana where years later Ernest Hemingway would draw inspiration. Eloy grew to love the place. He played in the colonial fort at the mouth of the bay, jumped off the pier, and swam in the turquoise waters. The sea thickened the air with a salty aroma that blew in the breeze up a sloping hill covered with houses and rusted their chain-link fences.

Eloy's family raised chickens, and he helped by feeding them and cleaning their coops. It was dirty work, but he didn't mind. He felt content to be free in this new country, and he reached manhood knowing that although he was born in Spain, Cuba was his home.

In the never-ending sameness of his cell, Eloy's thoughts wandered free. In this way, he told himself, he never stopped being a free man. He saw his imprisonment as an extension of the struggle for freedom that had taken the life of his brother Carlos. That was back in 1957, a decade earlier. Most Cubans knew the story of Carlos Gutiérrez Menoyo's death because it happened during one of the most daring acts of the revolution. Carlos had combat experience from the Spanish Civil War, and in World War II he had fought as part of the French army against the Nazis. Years later in Cuba, he became involved with the Revolutionary Directorate, a rebel group started by university students that was plotting to overthrow Fulgencio Batista. Carlos led a team that was to take over the presidential palace and kill Batista while a second team planned to seize the radio station CMQ.

On the afternoon of March 13, 1957, Carlos and his group arrived outside the palace in two cars and a red delivery truck. They stormed the building with assault rifles and grenades; Eloy stayed back, watching from outside. His job was to serve as a contact between Carlos's team and reinforcements.

Shots rang out as the attackers fired at soldiers and then ran upstairs to the president's office. They found it empty. Batista had gone upstairs to his living quarters, and the elevator that provided the only access remained stopped on the third floor.[3] The intruders were trapped. Bullets tore into the marble wall beside the main staircase as the rebels and guards exchanged fire. Many of the rebels were shot and fell just steps from a large room where on the frescoed ceiling an angel of Cuba was rising into heaven holding the nation's flag.

Eloy heard gunfire outside the palace as soldiers fired from the roof. He threw himself under a bus. Looking out from under it, he could see several rebels fleeing the building.

When the gunfire ceased, Eloy made his way behind parked cars to the nearby Palacio de Bellas Artes, where their backup force should have been waiting. No one was there. When tanks began to roll outside the palace, he fled.

The next day, Eloy went to Havana's Colón cemetery, where he found the bodies of thirty comrades awaiting burial. Eloy looked at the faces of the dead men; one of them was his brother.

Years later, just thinking of Carlos and the principles he stood for gave Eloy strength. Even in solitary confinement, Eloy remembered Carlos and felt sure he wasn't alone in his struggle.

4

Revolutionaries, "Modern Music," Havana Nights

At the United Nations in December 1964, Che Guevara declared that he felt patriotic not only as an Argentine and a Cuban revolutionary, but as a son of Latin America. If necessary, he said, "I would be prepared to give my life for the liberation of any of the countries of Latin America, without asking anything of anyone."[1]

It fit his ideal of the *Hombre Nuevo*, the New Man, who would work in solidarity with his countrymen, not for financial gain but rather for a higher cause—self-sacrifice for the common good and freedom from exploitation.

That spirit led him to the Congo, where he joined revolutionary forces, and later to Bolivia, where his small rebel group fought with the army but failed to win over the *campesinos* to its cause. With help from U.S. Green Berets and the CIA,[2] the Bolivian army tracked down the group, wounding and capturing Che in an ambush. He was executed by soldiers who drew lots to determine who would finish off the famous guerrilla lying on the floor of a small, run-down school.[3]

Ten days later, on October 18, 1967, Fidel Castro led a memorial cere-mony in Havana's Plaza de la Revolución. The crowd was so massive that it defied easy estimates. Some journalists estimated more than 500,000 people, while others looked out at the crowd filling the square under the glow of floodlights and calculated that nearly one million people had come to pay their respects.[4] A single bugler stepped to the microphone and played taps.

Paquito and the rest of the military band, who had been ordered back to Havana from a festival in Bayamo, sat on a platform above the crowd, waiting for their signal.

Paquito had once met Che briefly, and when the Argentine asked him what he did, Paquito said he was a musician.

"Music—no," Che replied. "I mean what sort of work do you do?"[5] The *comandante* intended it as a joke, but Paquito did not find it funny at all.

In Che's memory, the musicians put their lips to their instruments on cue and played a funeral march. Then came the national anthem with its famous lyrics "*morir por la patria es vivir*"—"to die for the fatherland is to live."

Fidel gripped the podium as he addressed the crowd, a giant portrait of Che behind him.

"The artist may die, especially when it's an artist of an art as dangerous as the revolutionary struggle, but what will not die in any way is the art to which he dedicated his life."

Fidel said Che had taken the ideas of Marxist-Leninism to their freshest, purest expression. And Che's blood, he said, "was spilled for all of the exploited, for all of the oppressed."

Che's spirit will live on in the revolution, Fidel said. "He left us his example."

Fidel continued: "If we want the model of a man, the model of a man who does not belong to our time but to the future, I say from the bottom of my heart that such a model, without a single stain on his conduct, without a single stain on his attitude, without a single stain on his behavior, is Che! If we wish to express how we want our children to be, we should say with all our hearts as vehement revolutionaries: We want them to be like Che!"[6]

The government put up billboards with images of Che and made slogans of his words, such as "All our action is a cry of war against imperialism." In time, every Cuban child was taught to recite a pledge in school to follow the ways of Che.

Nancy grew up respecting Che as an example of sacrifice, of someone who fought for a just cause. Around her neck she wore the blue-and-white bandanna of the *Pioneros* and recited their pledge in class each morning, repeating with the other children, "Pioneers for communism, we will be like Che!"

Bus depot in Santa Clara, 2005. (Ian James)

With six months of military service remaining, Paquito's professional life began to look up. Cuba was organizing a band of leading musicians, including pianist Chucho Valdés and guitarist Carlos Emilio Morales, with whom Paquito had played at the Teatro Musical. Paquito was tapped to play alto sax in a group of about two dozen. The Orquesta Cubana de Música Moderna was to be a showcase for Cuban talent, directed by Armando Romeu, the longtime musical director at the cabaret Tropicana. The choice of the term "modern music" reflected an uneasiness among some Culture Ministry officials with jazz—a music some still considered decidedly American. Whatever the higher-ups decided to call it, though, Paquito and his bandmates were glad they would be playing jazz.

Paquito's mother, meanwhile, was convinced "*ese barbudo*" was sending her country to ruin. She didn't see the use of attending meetings of the neighborhood Committee for the Defense of the Revolution, and whenever someone invited her, she replied, "I don't belong to anything because I don't have time," or "I have to dedicate my time to my children."

Maura's distaste for the system was so strong that she decided she had to leave the country with her seven-year-old daughter Rosario, even though Tito and her sons would stay. Paquito was nineteen when his mother secured permission to depart with the girl for Spain. When they left for the airport, Paquito stayed behind in his room and cried.

Maura took few possessions with her: a suitcase filled with clothes, about 2,000 pesos her mother had given her years before, and, of course, her wedding ring with its five tiny diamonds. It was no secret they were leaving for good. When the two stopped before a customs agent, he looked at the ring. "You have to leave it here," he said, telling her it belonged to the state. He confiscated the money too.

In Madrid, family friends helped Maura find work as a seamstress, and she eventually applied to travel to the United States, where she settled in New York with Rosario and found another job as a seamstress.

Back home in Havana, Paquito found the separation from his mother hard to take. At night, a neighbor sometimes heard him cry out in anguish: "*Why did you go away?!*"

In 1968, Paquito was able to leave Cuba for the first time in eight years when he was chosen to travel with a musical group on a tour of the Soviet Union, Bulgaria, Romania, and Hungary. In many places he visited, he noticed that governments were putting restrictions on people's personal lives. In Bulgaria, for instance, one musician complained that citizens had to request permission to move between cities. Paquito was struck by the lack of personal freedom in the Eastern Bloc.

He and the band visited Moscow's Red Square and the central shrine of Soviet communism, Lenin's tomb. The musicians waited in line to pay their respects before the embalmed body that lay under glass. When Paquito got close to the tomb, he declared loud enough for everyone to hear: "Damn, *maestro*, you've convinced me. . . ."[7] But of what Vladimir Ilyich Lenin had convinced him, Paquito didn't say.

Paquito was just as irreverent and mischievous back in Havana, perhaps more so. Years later, he recalled, "Havana nights have a peculiar aroma of sin from which it is difficult, if not useless, to detach oneself." On one of those nights, he and his date stepped out of a 1956 Oldsmobile with another couple, and the two pairs went their separate ways to be alone in the woods. Paquito and the young woman chose a secluded spot, where she slipped off her clothes in the moonlight and tugged at the zipper of his pants. Their clothes lay in a pile nearby when, moments later, a man appeared out of the bushes and shouted, "Hands up! You're under arrest, you *inmorales*. You know very well that this is prohibited!"[8]

As he shouted at them, the intruder picked up all their clothes, then disappeared into the trees. The lovers returned to Havana with little except their underwear.

The light moments of Paquito's life were interspersed with painful family experiences. When Tito Rivera secured government permission to leave the country, he packed his bags ahead of time and left them at the house of a relative to avoid having to say good-bye.

When his father left home, Paquito was sitting at a table writing music. His friend Félix Durán went with Tito to the airport to see him off. When Félix returned, Paquito appeared frozen in the same position, transfixed.

"Your father has just left," Félix told him. Paquito's eyes filled with tears as he heard what he already knew to be true.

By the time Paquito and his brother Enrique were left alone at home, they had learned like many Cubans to be resourceful and get by with whatever they had on hand. It was common for people to make their own replacement auto parts because they had no other choice. When some guitarists ran out of replacements for their highest-pitch string, they used telephone wire. Homemade solutions became the norm.

Paquito tried that approach with his family's house on Avenue 41A. The walls were dirty and desperately needed a paint job, but he and Enrique had no paint. So Paquito came up with another solution that he found amusing. He and Enrique covered the walls with pages from old magazines, newspapers, and posters that Paquito had picked up here and there, sticking all of it onto the walls with cassava starch. Their new wallpaper included colorful pages from the Polish magazine *Polonia*, which was published in Spanish and which Paquito liked because it included creative articles about art and music. The walls were plastered from top to bottom—a giant collage taking the place of paint. To add artistic flair, Paquito's friend Bobby Carcassés brought over a bit of purple paint and whitewash that he had, and stood on a stepladder in the hallway while painting the design of a fantastically tall, thin man playing the saxophone. Paquito was quite pleased with the new decor.

The neighbors learned they could expect just about anything from Paquito. Across the avenue from Paquito's house lived his friend Dinorah

Valdés and her younger brother Raulito, a flutist who practiced in a second-story room facing the street. Once when Raulito put his flute to his lips, he noticed that the instrument carried a mysterious echo. After each phrase, the sounds of an identical riff floated back. He played another passage, and the echo returned.

He looked out the window, and the mystery was solved. Across the street, Paquito stood by his front door, flute in hand, laughing uncontrollably.

5

Bloodshed, Letters Home, a Love Affair

Spain built Havana as a strategic port at the mouth of the Gulf of Mexico, a colonial way station to aid in the plunder of distant lands. It was a commercial center for selling tobacco and sugar produced with slave labor, and a stop-off point for galleons headed for Europe with loads of gold from Mexico and Peru. On a ridge overlooking the city from the opposite side of Havana Bay, the Spanish built one of several giant fortresses to guard their riches—Fortaleza San Carlos de la Cabaña. Atop its sloping stone buttresses were sentry boxes to help soldiers guard against any possible attack.

In the twentieth century, the fortress became a prison. Eloy spent many days and nights in the fort's belly with a group of prisoners in Galera 23A, a bare room with an arched ceiling and a single window. The stone walls of the cell often grew wet with the humidity.

At night, from the *paredón* in the fortress's dry moat, Eloy sometimes heard the shouts of the firing squad taking aim at condemned prisoners: *"¡Preparen! ¡Apunten! ¡Fuego!"* The shots rang out, and then there was silence.

Years earlier, Jesús Carreras and William Morgan, two of Eloy's top lieutenants, had fallen before firing squads at that same *paredón* wall. Sadness came over Eloy when he thought of them. They had been accused of being counterrevolutionaries and were executed less than two months after Eloy fled to Florida. Castro's government said they had been among hundreds leading an insurgency in the Sierra del Escambray, supported by airdrops of arms and supplies by the CIA. The two had denied any involvement.

After their deaths, some in Cuba portrayed Morgan and Carreras as villains. Che Guevara said Carreras had given Che's troops a cold reception in the mountains and recalled: "We saw in him an enemy."[1]

Morgan, a U.S. Army veteran who spoke accented Spanish, once said he joined the anti-Batista rebels "because I believe that the most important thing for free men to do is to protect the freedom of others."[2] After his death, some suggested he had come with the blessing of the CIA to help make Eloy an anticommunist alternative to Castro. Eloy insisted that was nonsense. He saw in the deaths of Carreras and Morgan the senseless elimination of two men who had fervently believed in the revolution.

They had grown close in the Escambray, where the mountains begin as rolling hills south of Santa Clara and rise to mist-shrouded peaks where coffee plantations flourish. This was the land of pine trees and rainbows that Eloy recalled in his prison songs and in letters to his daughter. He arrived there in November 1957 with a truckload of guns left over from the failed assault on the presidential palace.

There, in the crisp mountain air, Eloy learned for the first time how it felt to kill. It happened in 1958 on a ridge at Michelena. Seeing troops approaching, Eloy and about forty other rebels hid in bushes and trees to prepare an ambush. The soldiers outnumbered them by far. The troops came climbing up a slope toward the narrow pass, where they soon were hemmed in by a cliff on one side and a steep slope on the other. For Eloy's men, it was their third time in combat. The soldiers came closer and closer. Eloy crouched in the bushes, clutching his M3 rifle.

The soldiers were practically on top of them when the rebels opened fire. The soldiers had two choices: face the hail of bullets or take their chances jumping off the cliff. Some chose to jump.

When the gunfire stopped, the ground was littered with bodies. Eloy stood and began to survey the dead. As he approached the bodies of two soldiers lying face down, he noticed something odd. They were still holding their rifles, and Eloy saw a finger on a trigger. Aiming his rifle, Eloy stepped forward on a dry twig—snap! At the sound, the two rolled over and began to lift their rifles. Their faces were filled with terror in the instant that they realized Eloy would fire first. He pulled the trigger, and a hail of bullets shook their bodies.

Eloy during his rebel days in the Sierra del Escambray, late 1950s. (Courtesy of Patricia Gutiérrez)

The expressions on the soldiers' faces stayed frozen in Eloy's mind. One had opened his mouth in his last moment of life, and Eloy saw a gold tooth glimmering there. The look of terror in their eyes haunted him. Eloy consoled himself with the thought that if those men had lived, he himself would have died. That was war. He knew what he was fighting for, and someone had to die. So he fought on through the revolution, and still carried that hardened mental state years later in prison, naked but for his underwear and closed off from the world by the walls of his cell.

In Miami, Elena Patricia Gutiérrez grew up hearing Cubans speak admiringly of her father. He was so widely known that sometimes people simply called her *"la hija de Eloy."* Her aunts took her to meetings of Alpha 66, where she was placed before a microphone and sang the Cuban national anthem. The sympathetic crowd applauded and put dollar bills in a collection basket to support the anti-Castro fighters. At age six she was too young to fully grasp that she was being used.

Patricia, as friends called her, spoke English with her classmates at school. At home she spoke Spanish with her mother, who began working at a shoe store after Eloy left for Cuba. Patricia grew up much like any other girl in Florida, playing with dolls, riding merry-go-rounds, and watching the dolphin show at the Miami aquarium.

Because Eloy couldn't be with his daughter, he poured his spirit into letters to her. Inside the walls of La Cabaña on Valentine's Day in 1969, he wrote:

> I really wish I could hug you, give you a lot of kisses, see you laugh, play with you, hear your little voice and learn about your childhood things. You are very small still to be able to understand what all of this means for a father. I think in your innocence you won't understand the length of my absence. But I have faith that soon you will be able to hear my voice and that in simple words I will help you forget I was far away in the important years of your childhood and development, when a father is just as necessary as a mother. . . .

He thanked her for a letter on his birthday and urged her to study hard and be a good girl. He interspersed drawings with his handwriting to represent words—sketching the outline of Cuba midsentence to represent the island, peaks to represent mountains and so on.

> My *chiquitica*, I would like them to tell you many things about (Cuba), with the beautiful (flag) of the "Solitary Star," about the green countryside with its royal (palms), its rivers and (mountains), its coasts all lined with (beaches). Soon you will be older and then I will be near again to tell you in person the great history of this tropical country. I will tell you of "Hatuey," the good Indian whom they burned alive, of its great patriots who gave it everything. And why not? Also I'll tell you of the humble houses . . . of the tons of hungry children, without (toys) or opportunities to be able to learn what is written in (books). Knowing these things you will be able to know true love, and you will love all around you, you will feel happy in a life filled with feeling and glad to have been born.

Eloy drew a praying angel at the bottom of the page and closed the letter, saying: "Hundreds of kisses for you, from the one who loves you a lot and always remembers you. Eloy (*Papito*)."

With each passing year, Cuba's centrally planned economy was being focused more heavily on a single crop: sugar. It accounted for a large majority of exports, and many people across the country were involved in the harvest. A decade earlier, most of the sugar had gone to the United States. Now, with the embargo in place, much of the crop was bought by the Soviet Union.

In the history of Cuba's sugar industry, 1970 was to be a landmark harvest. Fidel Castro had been talking about it for years, predicting that in 1970 the island would produce 10 million tons of sugar and show the world the might of its socialist economy.

Reaching that production goal, he said, was a "matter of honor." Castro described the quest for 10 million tons as a battle that involved all Cubans. From the beginning of the harvest in October 1969, there would be no days off for cane cutters until they finished in July. The official holiday for Christmas was canceled.[3]

The government formed urban committees to prevent absenteeism and loafing during the harvest. Havana's nightlife all but disappeared. Nightclubs and cabarets closed, including—for a time—the Tropicana.

All of these were unwelcome developments for Paquito, who had been spending nights jamming at the waterfront nightspot Johnny's Dream. His look was decidedly unrevolutionary, with an Afro hairstyle, striped pants, and colorful shirts. When not playing music, he was listening to it, chatting with musicians in cabarets, watching the shows, or going out with dancers. To complain openly about the closing of the nightclubs could land him in trouble, so he only complained quietly among friends.

Despite the national campaign to produce 10 million tons of sugar, Cuba fell short. The harvest ended in July with more than 8.5 million tons of sugar produced—nearly one ton for each person on the island. Castro acknowledged defeat, but praised the country for its achievement and said the setback had brought lessons.

"Let us lift up our heads at this moment and confront our enemies," he said. "In this moment of failure let us go forward, revolutionary people, forward with renewed courage, with ever more intensity."[4]

The cabaret Tropicana, as seen by the author in 2001. (Ian James)

They were words that Castro himself seemed to live by. He had grown accustomed to staying one step ahead of successive U.S. governments and their clandestine efforts to bring him down. The CIA had tried to assassinate him by passing poison pills to the Mafia and by giving a pen-syringe to a Cuban agent. Once, U.S. agents even considered rigging a large seashell with explosives and setting an underwater booby trap at a spot where he liked to go skin diving.[5] Cuba's state security recorded hundreds of assassination plots over the years by various enemies. Castro proved cunning and resilient, often keeping his whereabouts a mystery.

Paquito was always eager to try something new in his music, so when the director of the Orquesta de Música Moderna stepped down, Paquito immediately volunteered for the job. But from the beginning it was clear he wasn't like other directors. In one of his first concerts, he quickly went into a passionate saxophone solo, then continued directing and started dancing on the stage. The dancing transformed into what looked more like the movements of an acrobat or a circus performer: Paquito jumped and lifted one foot in the air, then threw himself on the floor, got up again and whirled about. Watching his thin figure bounce around like that, the audience burst into laughter. The orchestra kept on playing.

Paquito found himself increasingly in the public eye as he performed with the orchestra. His flamboyant showmanship helped him charm admirers both on stage and off. After one concert for university students, he struck up a conversation with Eneida Pérez-Méndez, an architecture student who had offered to help watch the band's equipment until it could be picked up. The other musicians drifted away, but Paquito was impressed by Eneida and stayed behind chatting.

He asked her to come listen to him perform at a club later that night. She declined, saying she was tired. It was already nearly 1 a.m. They parted without exchanging phone numbers. But weeks later, through a friend of a friend, Paquito sent her a message. Eneida's friend Miriam told her, "Hey, Paquito D'Rivera is looking for you all over Havana. He wants you to go this Saturday to the Amadeo Roldán Theater. He's going to play."

So Eneida and Miriam went together. When they arrived, the show was sold out, so Eneida went backstage and asked around for Paquito.

"How great you came!" Paquito exclaimed, giving her a kiss on the cheek. "Well, and did you buy tickets yet?" he asked her.

"No, I thought it was your treat," Eneida said, somewhat surprised.

"Oh," Paquito said. "Don't worry. Wait here." He got Eneida and her friend into the show.

In a matter of months, Eneida and Paquito decided to marry. It was to be Paquito's second marriage. His first, to María de los Ángeles Córdova, a harpist, had been a struggle that lasted less than a year. With Eneida it was different. When they were together, it was as if they were children playing. They were married on June 20, 1971, at a civil registry in front of the Coppelia ice cream parlor's tree-shaded patio. Eneida, also marrying for the second time, wore a dress splashed with red, yellow, and violet that a friend had made for her. Paquito wore a tie cut from the same fabric and a suit he had bought in Poland. It was a small affair, witnessed by a few friends. The newlyweds settled into Paquito's family home, which his grandparents had built four decades earlier. On the window over the front door, there was an inscription with his grandmother's nickname and the year the house was built: "CUCA 1929."

While Paquito was largely satisfied with his personal life, he felt less so about his work with the orchestra. He tried to hold the musicians to high standards, though he was becoming frustrated that the band was being assigned to play backup for pop singers and variety shows. One evening, he was conducting while a Spanish singer performed, and the singer apparently thought the timing was off because he began to gesture as if to direct the band and increase the tempo. Paquito immediately noticed the intrusion, and to the audience's surprise intervened with a single, sweeping gesture of his baton that stopped the orchestra midsong. The theater fell silent.

That dismal experience reinforced Paquito's belief that the orchestra needed more opportunities to showcase its talent. "This band isn't for accompanying singers," he would say.

Paquito once got into trouble during a recording session when he blew a raspberry at the end of a song composed by *Comandante* Juan Almeida, a top leader of the revolutionary government. The raspberry ended up as part of the recording, and Paquito was questioned at length by his superiors who, although dismayed, decided Paquito hadn't meant it as an insult to the composer.

Paquito's volatile demeanor and critical attitude eventually landed him in trouble with officials in the Culture Ministry, who told Paquito it would be better for him to rest at home for a while. They said he wasn't being fired and would still receive his salary, but he wasn't welcome in the orchestra.

The rejection hit Paquito hard. He wasn't sure how to tell Eneida. He called Félix Durán and told him he had smoked a whole pack of cigarettes in one night. To Paquito, performing before a crowd was a physiological need, like breathing. Take that away, and he could never really be himself.

In 1972, Paquito was still trying to move beyond his bitter experience with the Orquesta de Música Moderna when Chucho Valdés approached him with an idea.

"Hey, *flaco*," the pianist said, using a nickname common for Paquito since he was rail-thin. "Oscar and I have an idea to form a little group and get out of that orchestra, which is so big that it's a major operation just to move it around."

The idea was to form a band with a select group of musicians that could more easily tour outside of Cuba.

"Talk less and play the same stuff that you've played up until now, or whatever you feel like playing," Chucho said. "We'll take care of the rest."[6]

The group took the name *Irakere*, meaning "jungle" in the language of the Yoruba people of Nigeria, and began making uniquely Cuban music—a fusion of Afro-Cuban rhythms with jazz, funk, and a bit of rock. Every afternoon, Paquito climbed onto a crowded bus carrying his saxophone and headed off to a school theater where the band would rehearse for about four hours.

In the capitalist world, he would later learn, few musicians could afford to commit so much time to perfecting their songs. But in communist Cuba, there was nothing but time.

6

Razors, Religion, Communist Youth

Behind the backs of their jailers, Eloy and other inmates secretly organized resistance groups, relaying messages however possible between cells and to relatives on the outside. When the authorities confirmed Eloy's involvement, he was tried, convicted, and sentenced to twenty-five more years, bringing his total sentence to fifty-five years.

Without hope of being freed, Eloy adapted his mind to the expectation that he would die in prison.

While held inside the fort Castillo del Príncipe, he and other inmates watched through a hole in their cell wall as some condemned prisoners were executed by firing squad in the courtyard. Eloy recalled one of them who shouted, "Down with communism!" before a bullet silenced him.[1]

For a time, the guards served only wheat gruel, morning and afternoon. For another stretch, it was macaroni at all feeding times. The men grew pale on their meager diet. Some got scurvy. Eloy developed an ulcer.

Through repeated hunger strikes, the prisoners were determined to draw attention to their needs. Eloy resisted the will to eat even when he could smell soup cooking in the prison galley. He and the other hunger strikers demanded books and better food—even just an egg or a piece of fish. In explaining the protests, Eloy would say, "We aren't asking for anything extraordinary. We're just asking that you give us the same treatment that Batista gave prisoners." He said this entailed being allowed to buy coffee and food, and being permitted books and a radio. Eloy felt the hunger strikes were having an effect in forcing the prison authorities to gradually make some concessions.

Eloy's father was able to visit periodically. Carlos was retired, living in an apartment on a busy thoroughfare in the Havana neighborhood of El Vedado. Eloy's mother had died years before in Miami, while his father had remained on the island, working for a time as a swimming pool manager and at a rayon factory. After Eloy's capture, his father immediately became a suspected accomplice and was jailed for months at El Príncipe. After his release, Carlos had to serve additional time under house arrest before he was eventually allowed to move freely again.

When Eloy's father visited the prison, he primarily brought news of the family—of Eloy's daughter in Miami, his sister Sarita in Spain, and his sisters Mercedita and Maritere in Miami. To see the two men together, it was obvious they were father and son. Each had the same lanky build and thin face. They also shared many ideas. Eloy's father was a quiet person, but he had strong views. A socialist, he felt the political system in Cuba defied simple description.

"We don't know what it's called," Carlos confided to one friend. "It has a little bit of socialism, a little bit of communism, and a little bit of Fidel. This is a creation of Fidel Castro."

For many years, Eloy's father applied to leave Cuba and return to Spain, but the government did not approve his exit papers. There was little he could do for his son except provide moral support whenever he visited. At the post office, he and others bought money orders in small amounts— ninety pesos, thirty-eight pesos, twenty-eight pesos—to send Eloy for cigarettes or anything else the authorities might allow him to buy. But often Eloy did not receive the money orders. When Carlos could, he brought his son chocolate bars, cigarettes, or razor blades.

Later, when Eloy's strong-headedness landed him in solitary confinement, the things the guards called "privileges," including visits from his father, were taken away. He stood alone in his dark, cramped cell. Only the slightest amount of light entered. A hole in the floor was the only bathroom.

In isolation, Eloy's beard grew back like it once had in the Escambray. He asked the jailers to give him a razor, but they refused—no matter how often he asked. He wondered angrily: Why should I be denied a razor?

So he determinedly grabbed a bit of hair between his fingers and yanked. The pain didn't stop him. He pulled his beard from his face strand by strand. When he was finished, the guards couldn't help noticing his swollen face. Without their assistance, and to spite them, he had shaved.

Cuba's Catholics had long worn medallions embossed with the image of their patron saint, the Virgin of Charity of Cobre. Others wore the colored beads of the Santería religion, paying homage to the powerful spirit of Changó or the love goddess Ochún. Religion was as much a part of Cuba as the tobacco plants that flourished in its soil. But after the triumph of the revolution, religion sometimes clashed with the generally atheistic principles of the revolutionary government.

In 1961, Fidel Castro announced that foreign priests who were waging a war against the revolution were no longer welcome and that private religious schools, which had been spreading the "poison of counterrevolution," would be brought under national control. Hundreds of priests left Cuba in the coming years. There were more than 700 priests on the island in 1960, many of them Spaniards, and five years later only 220 remained.[2] Nevertheless, Castro repeatedly linked his socialist principles with Christian theology and said the revolution was in no way opposed to religious concepts. He invoked Christ as an example, once saying: "He treated the poor the same as He treated the rich, and the black the same as the white. That society, to which He told the truth, did not want to forgive His preaching, and they ended up simply crucifying Him because He told them the truth."[3]

Practicing religion was permitted, but in some quarters it was frowned upon. Some of Castro's supporters accused the Catholic Church of favoring the bourgeoisie. It was as if religion had gone out of style. Nancy's parents were married in a church, but they never went to Mass in later years, and their daughter was never baptized. Christmas ceased to be an official holiday.

In Nancy's house, some Christmas traditions were carried on anyway, such as the family feast on the night of December 24, *Noche Buena*. Her grandfather Luis would set up a nativity scene complete with the three wise men, cows, and sheep. Nancy's father sometimes brought home a tropical pine tree he cut down on the edge of town. Other times, the family put up an artificial tree and decorated it with shiny baubles, tinsel, and cotton for a snowy effect.

Most everyone in Nancy's family—uncles, aunts, and cousins—would

Making a wish at the grave known as *La Milagrosa* in Havana, 2001. (Ian James)

come over on Christmas Eve wearing their best clothes and indulge in a feast of pork cooked with garlic, onions, oregano, and wine, served with generous portions of *yuca*, black beans, *maduros*, and rice. When it was available, Spanish *turrón* was served for dessert.

As Nancy grew older, the Christmas tree tradition faded, but the *Noche Buena* dinner always remained. It was a tradition that couldn't be extinguished, yet it was no longer religion. It was just family custom.

Cuba's government put a strong emphasis on education, creating a school system widely recognized to be among the best in the Americas. The government's commitment to schools was part of the same revolutionary philosophy that guided the nationwide literacy campaign of the early 1960s, which by official estimates reduced illiteracy from about 24 percent to 4 percent.[4] Some Cubans disputed those figures as a manipulation of reality, while others called the near-perfect literacy rate one of the revolution's greatest achievements.

Nancy, for her part, was a model student. She paid attention in class, did her homework, and frequently excelled. She looked forward to the daily recess when she would pay her five-cent piece, *un medio*, for crackers and a drink.

By the time she was ten, Nancy had a strong build and a tall frame that made her a top athlete. Noting her abilities, coaches chose her for the volleyball program at a special athletic elementary school where afternoons were dedicated to training. On the volleyball court, the girls lined up as the teacher called out instructions, then did warm-ups in unison. The afternoons passed with volleyballs bouncing in the air and girls blocking shots and lunging for digs.

Nancy was nearly five feet ten inches tall by the time she turned twelve. She was a solid asset to the volleyball team, but after two years of rigorous training she lost interest in the sport. Instead, when her two years at the special elementary school ended in 1974, she enrolled in a newly opened vocational school on the edge of Santa Clara that only admitted students with the highest grades.

The school, named after Che Guevara, was still under construction when its first classes began. Nancy attended her first year, seventh grade, in temporary classrooms set up nearby in Manacas. Food supplies at the school were meager, and the beans were so old that students occasionally found insects crawling in them. But Nancy didn't complain. Her parents visited every other weekend and brought plenty of home-cooked food. On the weekends when they didn't come, she traveled home by bus.

When Nancy began the eighth grade, she and her classmates transferred to the newly opened campus in Santa Clara along with hundreds of other students. They moved into simple quarters filled with bunk beds. The school was intended to prepare students not only in the classroom but also through volunteer work in the countryside. Nancy's class studied in the morning each day and then went to the *escuela al campo*, where they worked in the fields in the afternoon. School administrators told the students the revolution needed their help: they received free education, and in return they owed their work in the fields.

It was generally pleasant work, and the teenagers enjoyed themselves even as they walked across muddy fields. Adult guides tried to lead them in single-file lines, but the students were mischievous and sometimes ran away to hide among the crops.

Nancy and her classmates planted seeds, hoed, and watered the fields. They also harvested tomatoes, oranges, and sweet potatoes known as *boniatos*.

During the sweet potato harvest, students received instructions on how to divide the crop into three categories: 1) the most beautiful—for export; 2) the ones you could eat, but which weren't especially pretty—for consumption in Cuba; and 3) the ones you wouldn't eat—for the pigs.

Nancy was growing up at a time when the government was seeking to improve its central planning of the economy. Cuba had been divided into six provinces with few modifications since the Spanish drew boundaries on their colonial map in 1878. But with the passing of time, populations had shifted so much that the eastern province of Oriente had six times more people than the smaller central province of Matanzas. In addition, there were new pressures to reduce the geographic size of provinces as the government sought to improve regional administration and use its resources more equitably.

At a congress in December 1975, the Communist Party passed a resolution to redraw the map of Cuba. Instead of six provinces, there would be fourteen.[5]

"One of the principles of socialism is to search for the balanced development of the entire country," Fidel Castro explained the following year. "That is one of the fundamental principles of socialism, and we have to hold fast to that principle."

Nancy had lived in one of the largest provinces, Las Villas. Now the same area would include three new provinces: Sancti Spíritus to the east, Cienfuegos to the south, and the region where she lived, now called Villa Clara.

When Eneida graduated from the university, the government assigned her work as an architect in Matanzas, about an hour away from Havana by car. Paquito was frustrated about the idea of having her so far away, but what could he do?

Eneida's class held its graduation party at the cabaret Tropicana, and Paquito was among the musicians who performed. When he finished, Eneida led Paquito to a table to introduce him to some friends. The government's minister of construction also happened to be at the table, and someone introduced him to Paquito.

"Oh, nice to meet you," Paquito said. "You're the son of a bitch who wants to send my wife to Matanzas, right? And why don't you send yours?"

Eneida couldn't believe what had come out of Paquito's mouth. She scolded him later. But somehow he got away with it, and the ministry appointed Eneida to a job in Havana.

On the weekends, the two often traveled together to Paquito's gigs in Varadero, the strip of white sand beaches more than an hour's drive east of Havana where they had spent their honeymoon. They went to parties at musicians' houses, stayed up late, and sometimes slept on the floor.

Paquito was with his bandmates at a hotel in Varadero on March 28, 1975, when he was called to the phone. It was Alberto Romeu on the line with big news: Eneida had just given birth to a baby boy. Paquito rushed back to Havana the next morning. He walked into the hospital room and was delighted as he held the boy in his arms. They named him Franco.

Nancy was fourteen and in the eighth grade when the selection process began for students who would become members of the Juventud Comunista, the Communist Youth. A commission was instructed to choose only

the most disciplined and active students, singling them out as future leaders. Commission members checked on prospective students' behavior in
their neighborhoods and investigated how much their parents were
involved in the community. These were considered important factors
because future members of the Communist Party would be drawn from
the ranks of the Communist Youth.

From among about thirty students, twelve made the first cut. In the
end, four were chosen: two boys and two girls. Nancy and her friend Barbara were those two girls—"*militantes*," they would say, of the Juventud
Comunista.

At that time, they were very aware that their country could be a target
of violence. In October 1976, a bomb blew apart a Cuban passenger jet
shortly after it took off from Barbados, killing all seventy-three people on
board. Nancy watched on television as a memorial ceremony was held in
the Plaza de la Revolución. Photographs of the victims were displayed on
stands, while relatives broke down crying before the cameras. Hearses carried flag-draped coffins along avenues lined with crowds. Those killed
included twenty-three members of a Cuban youth fencing team returning
home after a tournament in Venezuela. Two men were arrested on suspicion of planting the bomb, and Castro said there was no doubt the CIA
was directly involved. Nancy felt disgusted by the horrific attack, seeing it
not only as evil but also as cowardly.

For the most part, though, she paid little attention to events outside
Villa Clara. Nancy and Barbara, like other girls in their class, were particularly excited to be approaching their fifteenth birthdays, a rite of passage
known simply as *los quince*. Reaching fifteen would mean they could shave
their legs, pluck their eyebrows, wear a bit of makeup, and begin a new
stage in life.

On the day of her party, Nancy went to a hairdresser, one of Barbara's
cousins, who shaped her hair into flowing curls. Nancy's family rented her
a mauve dress of satin and tulle, and in her hair she wore cloth flowers.

Neighbors helped prepare the house for the party. Flowers were laid on
the dining room table. The family ordered a towering three-level cake with
garlands of white frosting. Nancy posed for a photographer, in some shots
smiling with lips closed and in others revealing her teeth. She posed with
her parents for a toast.

Nearly all thirty students in her class showed up for the party. Many

Nancy on her fifteenth birthday, 1977. (Courtesy of the Lledes family)

girls brought their mothers, and the crowd filled her house. Beer and rum punch were served, and the teenagers danced in the living room to popular ballads. Not everyone who showed up had been invited, however. When Nancy's father spotted a stranger—a young man with long hair and a golden chain around his neck—he grabbed the boy by the arm and led him to the door. Nancy was sorry to see him go, but the party quickly resumed and lasted until midnight.

7

A Jazz Cruise, a Mountain Hike, a Prison Tale

Across the Florida Straits, the U.S. presidential elections of 1976 brought new possibilities of change in the American government's entrenched, hard-line stance toward Cuba. Jimmy Carter, who won the race, said while campaigning that relations could improve "on a measured and reciprocal basis."[1]

Diplomatic relations still weren't restored, and no high-level talks were scheduled. But in 1977, the United States opened an Interests Section in Havana, a first step toward resuming some limited diplomatic dialogue. The Cubans did the same, opening an Interests Section in Washington. A Cuban-American banker, Bernardo Benes, represented Carter's government in a series of secret meetings with Castro and his top aides. One of the major points that Benes pressed was the release of political prisoners, including Eloy Gutiérrez Menoyo.[2] Other diplomats and politicians had been asking for his release for years, but none had yet convinced Castro.

With the slight easing of tensions came a new opportunity. A group of American musicians quietly arranged to travel to Havana on what was billed a "Jazz Cruise." The star-studded list of passengers included Dizzy Gillespie, Stan Getz, Earl "Fatha" Hines, and David Amram. They traveled in a group of more than 300 Americans, setting sail from New Orleans on a Greek ship, the M.S. *Daphne*. Such a thing had not happened since Castro came to power some eighteen years earlier.

As the ship neared the Cuban coast on May 17, 1977, passenger Arnold Jay Smith—a writer and jazz aficionado—noticed Cuban gunboats speeding out to meet the vessel. They escorted the ship as it passed the colonial fort El Moro and drifted into Havana harbor. The passengers streamed down the pier and headed for the city. Hundreds of cheering Cubans awaited them in the street. Gillespie stopped to talk in English with the people. Few recognized the famous trumpeter at first, but word soon got around as to who he was. "There is the artist, he is the artist," someone in the crowd said excitedly.[3]

News of the cruise ship's arrival spread quickly through the city, but Paquito had heard nothing about it when he walked up to his front door that day and spotted a note, written in pencil on a scrap of a brown paper bag. It was a mix of Spanish and English and said something like "*Hola* Paquito, *Vine* lookin' for you, *pero no estabas*. See ya soon! Dizzy Gillespie."

Paquito looked around, at first suspecting a prank. But it wasn't. Paquito's bandmate Arturo Sandoval had picked up the legendary trumpeter in his car and had taken him for a ride, stopping by Paquito's house.

Dizzy was interested in meeting the all-star members of Irakere, who by that time had become popular in Cuba with their first recording, "*Bacalao con pan*," a unique style of music with danceable Afro-Cuban rhythms and a jazzy feel.

The day after the Americans arrived, the Culture Ministry arranged for them to meet Irakere. They gathered in the cabaret Caribe at the Hotel Havana Libre. Paquito was thrilled to join the visitors. With the chairs still upside down on the tables in the empty cabaret, the musicians launched into an impromptu jam session. Smith, who later wrote about the visit in *Billboard* magazine, taped the session. He felt it was an important moment in jazz history.

Arturo Sandoval played his trumpet with such precision and power that Dizzy pulled off a tablecloth and waved it in the air as if to surrender. Dizzy then joined Paquito in an interpretation of a Charlie Parker tune. Smith listened to Paquito as his fingers danced on the alto. His training was clearly classical. "As soon as you heard it, it had a perfect, round sound," Smith later recalled. Writing in *Billboard*, he said of Paquito's performance, "There was the bite of Cannonball Adderley, facility of Charlie Parker, and warmth of Benny Carter."[4]

Later, relaxing in the pool at the Hotel Nacional, Dizzy remarked to Paquito how much he admired his country.

"I love Cuba and this revolution," he said.

"So why don't you stay here then?" Paquito asked.

"No, there's too much money to make in America still," Dizzy replied. They laughed politely, and the conversation strayed from politics.

The ship departed, Arnold Jay Smith took his recording back to New York, and Paquito was honored to have become friends with Dizzy and the other renowned musicians. The outside world was beginning to take notice of Irakere and Paquito D'Rivera.

One day at home in New York, Maura received a call from Paquito's brother Enrique from Cuba. Her son was calling from his aunt's house because he feared government spies were recording the family's conversations. He tried to relay his message without mentioning a name: "*Mami*, someone you love very much is going to Canada."

Maura became so nervous that she hung up and exclaimed to her teenage daughter, "Rosi, Rosi! Paquito is going to Canada!"

"What part of Canada?" she asked.

"Ay, I didn't ask! I don't know," Maura said. "Don't worry. I'll find out." Calling back, Maura asked Enrique, "Those friends of yours, where in Canada are they going?"

"Montreal."

Maura hung up and told her husband, "Let's go to Montreal right now."

"But you didn't get the address?" Tito asked incredulously.

Enrique wasn't able to give it to her, she explained. "Don't worry. I'll look once we're there. Let's go to Montreal."

The family loaded their bags into their 1964 Chevrolet and headed off. Tito protested the whole way, saying, "My God, this woman must be crazy—such a big city, and without an address or telephone number."

Maura, her cousin Panchú, Rosario, and Tito checked in to a hotel in Montreal and began calling around to other hotels to see where Irakere might be staying. After hours of calling, and without any clues, they set out in the car again. It was about seven in the evening. Rosario drove, and Maura scanned the sidewalk along a downtown avenue for any sign of the Cubans. Then Maura spotted them—two men peering into store windows.

"Rosi, those two *negros* are Cubans!" Maura declared. In the back seat,

Tito put his hands on his head and declared, "Now this woman really has gone crazy, but it's my fault for following her."

Rosario got out of the car, walked toward the men and asked them, "*Oigan, ¿ustedes son cubanos?*"

Tito had opened the car window to watch, and one of the musicians exclaimed, "Tito Rivera, *coño*, how great it is to see you after so many years." He then went on to explain that Paquito was with their group down the street. The musician pointed. "Look, you see that Pepsi-Cola sign there? That's where we left him behind."

Rosario double-parked outside the cafeteria with the Pepsi sign and hurried in. She met several Cuban women who were dancers from the cabaret Tropicana, where Enrique performed in the band. Paquito had already left the cafeteria, but one of the dancers soon found him and told him, "Hurry, your mother is looking for you like crazy!" She warned Paquito to be careful because security agents were all around, but pointed to where he could meet his family. "They are on that corner, behind the church," she said.

Paquito hadn't seen his mother or sister for a decade, and it had been nearly as long since he had seen his father. They all hugged tearfully. Maura felt there was no denying that the hand of God had helped bring about this moment.

They spent a week together. Paquito's family would pick him up a few blocks from his hotel to avoid arousing the suspicion of his minders, and would bring him to their hotel, where they talked for hours and joked. They were visits of both joy and sadness. Paquito thought his mother seemed the same as always, but his father appeared gloomy and worn down. He hadn't adapted well to life in New York, and he smoked perpetually.

Maura tried not to mention politics. Nevertheless, Paquito confided that he didn't care for the system in Cuba. "All of that is unbearable," he explained vaguely, "but since you have to make do. . . ."

Eneida, who wasn't permitted to travel outside Cuba with Paquito, remained at home with their son Franco. Maura never suggested to Paquito that he should leave them. She knew how hard it had been to leave behind her own family when she went to Spain.

One of the most terrible effects of prison life was the way the long silences seemed to empty the human mind of language. Eloy felt his vocabulary slowly slipping away. Sometimes when he needed something, such as a towel, he couldn't find the word for it.[5] It just wasn't there.

Even so, at least one prisoner on the cellblock usually had a rudimentary radio pieced together with a wire coil and took on the duty of listening to the latest news. Sometimes an inmate would repeat the news out loud. Other times, someone wrote down the report using pencil and paper and passed the note around.

In the frequent silence of their cells, the men knew little of the massive lobbying effort being waged internationally for the release of political prisoners. After many hours of talks with the go-between Bernardo Benes, Castro eventually agreed to release prisoners who had committed crimes against the state or had been convicted of crimes committed during the Batista regime. On the night of October 20, 1978, Benes flew to Havana with several Cuban-Americans on a highly publicized trip to bring back the first group of political prisoners.[6]

The Cuban government also arranged a meeting with Eloy inside Combinado del Este prison the next morning. Anticipating that possibility, Benes had brought Rafael Huguet, a building contractor and close friend of Eloy who lived in Miami and had once joined in his hit-and-run raids off the Cuban coast.

Guards brought Eloy into the prison warden's office, where the Cuban-American visitors, reporters, and others were assembled. When Rafael saw Eloy's thin figure, he called out to him and stepped forward. But Eloy recoiled and raised a hand as if someone was going to strike him. A moment later, he realized it was his friend and exclaimed, "Huguet!" They embraced. Eloy remained wary about the aims of their visit. But then, with journalists and cameras in the room, Eloy began to speak words that he knew the outside world would hear. He motioned to three military officers who were standing to the side and said they could not be trusted, suggesting they served as undercover informers. "These men don't even know their names, because they change them every day." Eloy said Castro could have released the prisoners long ago, and that dialogue with him wasn't the answer.[7]

That night, the first 46 prisoners of more than 3,600 who were deemed political prisoners flew to Miami on a charter flight.[8] Eloy wasn't among them. His sharp comments cost him. Back in his cell, he recalled what

Huguet said to him as he left: "I'm going to try to come see you again. Let's see if they let me."

Some time before Huguet's visit, Eloy had noticed that the government was making some limited improvements in the prisons, allowing inmates to keep more personal items, such as pens and pencils. Over a period of months, Eloy patiently collected paper, pens, colored pencils, and other supplies.

As he thought about his friend's pledge to return, Eloy decided he would write a story for his daughter and ask Huguet to smuggle it out. He set to work in his cell with a pen and small sheets of onion-skin paper, writing in a tiny cursive that filled the pages in perfectly symmetrical lines:

> Sitting on the roof of the old stone house, Antonio scanned the distance in all its immensity. His young face bore a trace of infinite sadness. His pain was immense. He understood that the possibilities were remote, perhaps impossible. But he needed to believe. He stubbornly held on to a slight hope. And that was what kept him there directing his untiring gaze over the waves . . . and he waited . . . like someone waiting for a miracle. One after the other the memories came and they all revolved around the same thing. Yes, that same thing! . . . he would return.[9]

Antonio was waiting for the return of an unusual bird with black feathers that some time ago had surprised the men in their remote island camp.

Though the story was fantasy, it was set in scenes from Eloy's past. The island camp resembled Eloy's old base in the Bahamas, and as he wrote he drew on memories of a bird his group had encountered there.

The men in the story were armed for their fight against "totalitarianism," and they joked among themselves about the odd bird hanging around their camp: "It's an infiltrator sent by the dictatorship. It must be interrogated."

Quickly they learned to get along with the newcomer, feeding it and eventually giving it its own plate. The bird became a companion for the men. It watched them fishing from a skiff, and eventually led them to the fish.

When Antonio went off to sea alone on a trip for supplies, he got lost. The other men searched for him in vain, and the bird kept flying over the sea looking for him. One day the bird arrived back at camp with a note tied to its leg from Antonio, whose boat had broken down. "I lost my instruments and don't know my position," he told his comrades, whom he referred to as his "dear brothers of the struggle."

"I haven't seen a boat for days, which means that I'm outside navigational routes," Antonio said in his note. The men were overjoyed that the bird had brought the letter. In that moment, they finally came up with a name for the seabird—*Radarista*, the radar man. "Long live the *Radarista!*" they shouted. At daybreak, the bird led a search party to Antonio. It was just in time, because if he had continued drifting, Eloy wrote, "Antonio would have been captured by the enemy patrol."

Returning to their small island, the men held a banquet in honor of the *Radarista*. The bird stayed with them, often flying out to greet any arriving boats. Once while Antonio was swimming, he saw what he thought was the dark form of a shark and swatted at it with a piece of wood. What he hit turned out to be the bird, which was underwater and just about to surface. Eventually the bird recuperated and flew off into the sky, circling above the camp. Antonio, with tears in his eyes, shouted for the bird to come back. But it didn't. "The *Radarista* was lost on the horizon forever."[10]

Between writing sessions, Eloy hid the small pages by rolling them up and carefully sliding them into a hole in the wall. When he finished, the story was forty pages long. Putting on the finishing touches, Eloy made a cover with thin cardboard, and he partly melted wax paper to stick it to the outside. Using colored pencils, he wrote the title *El Radarista* on the cover and drew a scene with the island camp showing a bird atop a stone house.

He sewed in the pages with four even stitches, using fine string, and on the title page he wrote: "To my daughter Elenita on her birthday. La Habana, 1977." It was actually 1978, but Eloy overlooked that detail. His daughter had turned sixteen earlier that year.

Eloy hid the little book and waited for Rafael Huguet to come back. It didn't take long. He returned as expected in November 1978 as part of the "Committee of 75," a group of exiles chosen to meet with Castro in an effort to open dialogue. The guards never suspected that Eloy had the small booklet hidden in his underwear, which he wore with only a T-shirt.

A guard handed him a pair of pants to put on before leading him out to meet his visitor.

Eloy was taken to Villa Marista, a former Catholic school that had been converted to a state security building and contained rooms used for questioning suspects. Eloy was led to a room where he met his old friend, and they embraced. Supposing the conversation was being recorded, Eloy looked around, pulled back a curtain, and found the wires of recording equipment dangling from an open space in the wall. Quietly, he pointed out the wires to Rafael.

As he pulled out the booklet, Eloy asked him, "How is my daughter? Have you been able to see her?"

Rafael said she was fine and was growing up. Eloy grasped the booklet and put it into his friend's hands, saying, "Well, give her a hug for me."

The book made its way to Patricia. Years later, as she lobbied for her father's freedom, she published his little book.

Irakere was quickly gaining a following in the jazz world. Shortly after the jazz cruise visited Havana, the president of CBS Records, Bruce Lundvall, arranged a visit to hear Cuban musicians and in particular Irakere. A law firm arranged the visas for him and several others. They flew to Havana through Montreal. After meeting with officials from the Culture Ministry and going through initial formalities, the Americans were invited to an outdoor concert where Irakere was playing before a few hundred guests. Lundvall would later say he was "blown away" by the band. The recording executive felt he had to find a way to sign the group, which was difficult due to the U.S. embargo.

The Cuban government eventually agreed that any royalties from record sales would go into a blocked account to cover the expenses of other Cuban musicians traveling in the United States. Once the deal was done, Irakere made plans to go to New York that summer to record an album and perform live.

On this trip, Paquito visited his family openly at their apartment across the Hudson River in Union City, New Jersey. The eleven-member band recorded their album *Irakere* on July 5, 1978, at a studio on Thirtieth Street, taping nine songs including Chucho's masterful "*Misa Negra*." The recording soon caused a sensation with its fusion of jazz, salsa, and rock set to Cuban rhythms. It was the first time many Americans had heard

Paquito jamming with Chucho Valdés in Finland, 1977.
(Courtesy of Paquito D'Rivera)

this type of music, and it was quite possibly the first album recorded in the United States by musicians living in Cuba under Castro's government.[11]

Soon after the recording session, Irakere made its concert debut at Carnegie Hall. They were the last act of the night and were supposed to go on after a bill of pianists including Mary Lou Williams and Bill Evans. The Cubans had tremendous respect for the grand old hall and were honored to be performing there. Paquito often appeared relaxed before shows, but this time was different. His parents were going to be in the audience, as were Dizzy Gillespie, Tito Puente, and so many others. Irakere's guitarist,

Carlos Emilio Morales, usually carried a flask of rum with him to help calm the jitters, and he had it with him that night when he ran into Paquito in the men's restroom backstage.

"Hey, I'm nervous," Paquito said, looking ill. "Give me a little taste."

Carlos Emilio handed Paquito the flask, and he took a swig. It was the first time Carlos Emilio had seen his bandmate in such a condition.

Standing before the crowd, Bruce Lundvall introduced Irakere, which was not listed in the playbill. A few in the audience who favored softer, acoustic jazz stood and walked out when they heard Irakere's explosive style. Many others stayed.

Paquito spotted his parents on a balcony next to Chucho's father, pianist Bebo Valdés. Seeing them boosted his spirits, and his powerful riffs filled the hall. The songs, mostly written by Chucho, swirled and pounded with an uncommon rhythm and style. As the band played on, Lundvall realized if the show didn't end shortly, workers at Carnegie Hall would by contract have to be paid for another day's work. But he decided it didn't matter; CBS Records would pay them. He stood and announced the show would continue. Dizzy Gillespie and Stan Getz joined the band on stage, turning the performance into an elaborate jam session of the highest caliber. At the end of the show, the musicians stepped down from the stage and paraded through the aisles playing and dancing.

The visit was an unprecedented success, and Irakere won a Grammy for the Best Latin Album of 1979.

At the time, Spanish Prime Minister Adolfo Suárez was lobbying the Cuban government to release any Spaniards held as political prisoners. Eloy's father Carlos wasn't exactly a prisoner, but he had been trying to leave Cuba for years. Finally the government gave him permission, and he left for Spain. Once there, he traveled to Oviedo to be with his daughter Sara. Writing to a friend in February 1979, he remarked that he had flown to Madrid, the city where he was born, "on the same plane that the royals use for their travels."

He recalled how he was greeted at the airport by an avalanche of reporters and photographers. The next day, he was able to read what had been written in the papers. One headline said simply, "One left." As Carlos put it in his letter, "now there is only one left, my son." By the time Carlos arrived in Oviedo, his daughter had received a letter from the Spanish government saying Eloy's freedom was pending and his prison conditions had improved.

"We are all waiting for him," Carlos wrote. "The weather here is very cold and the snow received me in abundance, but the houses have heating and there are plenty of blankets and more blankets, and as for clothing it's one sweater on top of another and plenty of wool, and when going out in the street an overcoat, scarf and gloves."

Shortly afterward, Eloy's father died. He was eighty-seven.

An army colonel visited Eloy at the prison to bring him the news. Fidel even sent his condolences.

At the end of the 1970s, many Cubans in small towns still considered a bus ride to Havana a long journey. Paquito was among the elite few who had permission and the financial backing to travel internationally. His passport was filled with stamps from countries such as Yugoslavia, Switzerland, and Finland. Irakere had traveled to Angola to perform for Cuban troops fighting in its civil war. The band also went on tour in the United States, opening rock concerts for Stephen Stills.

At home in Cuba, jazz had become more accepted. Early in 1979, CBS Records and the Cuban government arranged for a music festival called the Havana Jam. A long list of artists and bands from overseas came for three nights of concerts at the Karl Marx Theater. The musicians included Weather Report, Billy Joel, Dexter Gordon, Héctor Lavoe, and Rubén Blades. During the festival, a visiting journalist writing for *Billboard* magazine, Eliot Tiegel, asked Paquito what life was like for a musician in Cuba.

Paquito replied in accented English that the government didn't tell him what to play. "I play what I want," he said. "It's a comfortable life. You can work easy. I think it's good because we have no worry about money. . . . The government pays you for rehearsals and each month you receive your salary."[12]

Being a star allowed Paquito to have extra privileges. The government arranged to sell him a car, a yellow Soviet-made Lada, which meant he no longer had to travel on crowded buses with his instruments. He was so widely known that he could walk into almost any hotel in Havana—places usually reserved for foreign tourists—and be welcomed.

"To Paquito, no one could say no," Eneida said years later. "The whole world knew Paquito."

Sometimes the couple met after work and went to a hotel, where Paquito threw himself into the pool, took a swim, and then lounged at the poolside with a beer, next to his wife. Relatives or friends served as babysitters for their son when they couldn't be with him.

In those years, Cubans waited in line at state-run markets to obtain bread, eggs, cooking oil, ham, and various other items. Milk was rationed and mainly given to children seven years old and younger. The government had converted military barracks to schools and had invested large sums in health care, but the socialist system still struggled to provide some basic goods for Cubans.

Paquito usually joked and laughed about Cuba's troubles. But deep down, he was becoming frustrated with a system that he felt held him back. At the same time, he found it difficult to imagine leaving the country.

"I'm at the peak of my life," Paquito told his friend Alberto Romeu one day while they sat talking in Alberto's living room.

"No, you're just on the first floor of the building, so it's up to you how many floors your building is going to have," Alberto told him. "You have to get out of Cuba to build the rest of your building. Outside Cuba, there are no limits."

Paquito thought about what his friend had said. He now earned about 500 pesos a month as a member of Irakere, a large sum for a Cuban but nothing compared to musicians in other countries. While at home at night, Paquito expressed himself as he wrote music, drawing on jazz, classical, and traditional Latin styles. He composed and arranged pieces at a table near the sink, not far from the bucket where the family stored water for when the faucet ran dry. His music consumed his attention and energy. He could hear the tunes in his mind.

Paquito yearned to play a greater repertoire of jazz, to grow musically as a soloist, and to live with more freedom. The urge wasn't quite enough to make Paquito leave. But before long, events began to push him toward a decision.

At the end of the school year, Nancy and several hundred classmates departed on buses for their graduation trip to the Sierra del Escambray. They were going to hike to the spot where Che Guevara once had a rebel camp known as Caballete de Casa. The seventeen- and eighteen-year-olds were accompanied by guides and Red Cross doctors.

When the bus reached the foot of the mountain, Nancy stepped off wearing boots and carrying a canteen. She and the other students hiked through lush forests and terraced coffee plantations while mules trailed behind carrying their food. Here and there alongside a river, the teenagers picked *pomarosa* fruit from the trees. They enjoyed eating its fragrant white flesh as they hiked along, tossing aside the seeds.

By evening, the group reached camp. The girls slept on blankets under the roof of a simple shelter, while the boys slept under the trees. The next morning, they set out again on their trek and quickly worked up a sweat. The forest's dense canopy stretched over their path and brought welcome shade to the hikers. Wanting to cool off more, Nancy and several classmates took a dip in a stream. Clear water gushed out of cracks in the mountainside along the trail, spilling in sheets down the rock. Nancy pressed her canteen against the rock to catch some of the water, which tasted wonderfully pure.

When the path grew steep, the hikers grabbed branches and hanging vines to steady themselves. They reached the mountaintop in the afternoon and rested among palm-thatched huts that stood at the spot where Che was thought to have had his camp. They sang the national anthem, and then fell silent as their principal led them in a ceremony to honor Che.

Nancy saw Che as a man who fought selflessly for a just cause, and it seemed fitting to her that they remembered him for his sacrifice. No one mentioned that Eloy Gutiérrez Menoyo had led another rebel group fighting in the mountains nearby. Nancy had never heard of him.

8

Mariel

On April 1, 1980, six Cubans in a commandeered bus crashed through the gates of the Peruvian Embassy in Havana, seeking asylum. Armed Cuban guards were posted outside the embassy, and gunfire erupted in the confusion.[1] The battered bus came to a stop partially inside the compound, with a piece of the fence lying beneath its wheels. One guard lay on the ground bleeding from the chest. The people on the bus had no weapons, and it was apparent the fatally wounded guard had been hit by either a stray shot from another guard or perhaps his own ricocheting bullet.[2]

Peru declined requests by the Cuban government to turn over those who had plowed through the gates. In response, Cuba removed its guards from their posts around the embassy and used bulldozers to demolish their sentry boxes. They also hauled away boulders that had been placed in driveways as a deterrent to others.[3]

The Communist Party newspaper *Granma* announced the decision on its front page: "We cannot protect embassies that do not cooperate in their own protection."

It appeared Fidel Castro was trying to inconvenience the embassy by allowing more dissidents inside. But the mass of people that converged on the embassy clearly exceeded his expectations. First about fifty entered the compound. By the next day, more than 2,000 had jammed into the grounds, trampling the embassy's lawns and gardens. On April 6, more than 10,000 people were packed inside, pushing up against the chain-link fence.[4] Some even found space on the roof.[5]

Party loyalists organized a giant counterdemonstration, going door-to-door urging others to join the march. Workplaces were ordered closed, and all who backed the government were expected to show their support by attending the march. In the crowd stood Paquito with Eneida and their five-year-old son. They held signs handed out by organizers, with slogans such as "Let the scum leave!"[6] Paquito didn't say it, but in the spectacle he felt something was terribly wrong.

The United States, Spain, Peru, and Costa Rica soon agreed to accept asylum seekers. Buses shuttling the first people from the embassy to Havana's airport were pelted with stones. In the streets, people shouted at those in passing buses, "We don't want you!" Planes full of refugees began leaving for Costa Rica. Many asylum seekers went on to Peru.

Then, with little explanation, the Cuban government halted the airlift. Castro said exiles in Miami could bring boats to the port of Mariel to pick up those who wanted to leave.

Hundreds of boats soon crowded into the harbor to pick up the deserters. Anger against those who decided to leave flared as defenders of the revolution went to defectors' homes and threw stones and rotten eggs at their doors and windows while they cursed the traitors as *gusanos*, or worms. The gatherings were called *mítines de repudio*, or condemnation rallies. Militant Communist Party supporters confronted those who tried to defect, painting their houses with insults, beating some and spitting at others who dared to face their accusers.

Paquito's brother Enrique was among those seen as a traitor. Earlier in the year, the U.S. Interests Section had approved a visa for him to travel to New York. The response was swift. He was kicked out of the orchestra at the Tropicana, where he played saxophone, and was relegated to carrying instruments. He was still waiting for Cuba to grant his exit permit when the Mariel boatlift came. Paquito feared that would make his brother a suspect. As rumors swirled that neighbors would come to harass his brother, Paquito felt angry and desperate.

"I can't take any more," he told one friend. Paquito wanted to leave, but he knew the authorities would never let him step onto a boat in Mariel Bay. There seemed to be no easy solution. Paquito didn't want to leave behind Eneida and Franco, but he didn't see any other option. So he began to devise a plan. He would have to go alone when no one expected it. Irakere's upcoming tour to Scandinavia, with a layover in Madrid, provided the opportunity.

On a park bench in Havana one morning, Paquito sat talking with Eneida and a friend about his plans. Eneida didn't want him to leave

alone. They had discussed the possibility of Eneida going on her own, perhaps pretending to be a lesbian since the rumor was that homosexuals
were being permitted to leave in large numbers through Mariel. Their son
Franco could leave with Paquito's brother Enrique so as not to arouse suspicion. But Eneida said she was afraid. She worried that as a government-
trained architect, she would be stopped.

All the options seemed fraught with pitfalls. Eneida feared that if
Paquito left, they might never be together again. As they continued talking
on the park bench, it became clear there was no middle ground. Their
tempers flared and Paquito stood up. The conversation ended in shouting.

Grudgingly, Eneida eventually agreed that Paquito should go alone. She
wanted the best for him.

"If we meet, we meet again," she said. And if not, at least Paquito
would achieve his goals. If he didn't go, Eneida thought, he would probably live out the rest of his life as a frustrated musician. Paquito felt he had
reached the ceiling of success in Cuba—Irakere was the top, and he
wanted to achieve more on his own.

"I can't live here anymore," he later recalled thinking. "I need wider
horizons. I need to prove myself in a tougher scene, where people really
blow on these instruments and know what really happens."[7]

The day before his flight, Paquito stopped at the home of his friend
Alberto, who mentioned his view that even the island's top musicians
always had to wait for official approval to do what they wanted. "You have
no future here," he concluded. "You should go."

Alberto's words struck a chord. Paquito said farewell and returned
home more convinced than ever. But it was to be a long night. Years later,
Paquito recalled the fear he felt that night when he heard a condemnation
rally just a block away outside a neighbor's home. He worried they would
come next for Enrique. He had covered the front window with a piece of
plywood just in case. When Paquito spotted some of the people walking
down the block toward his house, he took out a foot-long tribal knife he
had brought back from Angola and burst out into the street with a crazed
look in his eye, brandishing the double-edged blade and shouting out that
he was staying in Cuba and wouldn't tolerate any scene outside his house,
much less any harassment of his brother.

The crowd he feared never materialized, but Paquito couldn't sleep that night. The decision pained him. He didn't want to leave Eneida and Franco behind, and he hoped they would be together again soon.

Paquito filled his suitcase with sticks, bricks, an old boot, and another old suitcase. There was no sense in taking anything he really needed because he planned to desert the band during their stopover in Madrid, and the unnecessary suitcase would continue on to Scandinavia. By packing the bag, he also convinced himself there would be no turning back. No one in the band knew about his plans.

When he got out of the car at Havana's airport early on the morning of May 6, he didn't hug his wife or kiss his son. He couldn't cry.

Eneida stood with Franco and the other musicians' wives on the terrace overlooking the runway. All she had told the boy was that his father was going on a trip. She couldn't show her pain.

Paquito climbed the steps to board the plane. He turned, looked toward his family, then raised his hand in a big wave, and was gone.

In her first year at the university, Nancy found her true loves: chemical engineering and a fourth-year electrical engineering student named Federico Falcón. Nancy, a serious and disciplined student, often walked briskly to the cafeteria at lunchtime carrying her books. Federico, a basketball player who stood taller than most students, noticed her moving through the crowd as he chatted with friends. She caught his attention because she, too, was tall and athletic. Her good looks and wavy black hair stood out.

Federico eventually found the courage to follow Nancy to the lunch line, where he struck up a conversation.

"Have I seen you before somewhere?"

"No, I don't know you," she said.

Nancy knew what he was up to, and she played along. He invited her to a party. She said no. But before long, the two became friends. Fico, as he was called, liked Nancy's quiet, modest nature. She liked the way he was talkative and always seemed to make her laugh.

Fico had already been through one relationship and had separated. The woman lived in Santa Clara with their son, Franklin. Now Fico was on his own again. He had spent his adolescence with adoptive parents because his mother died young and his father had left for the United States years before. Fico didn't have regular contact with his father, and while growing

Nancy at Uvero, late 1970s. (Courtesy of the Lledes family)

up he never thought seriously about leaving Cuba. But as a young man, he wondered what it would be like to live in the United States. He asked his new girlfriend what she would do if one day he decided to leave. "Would you go with me?"

She gave a firm no. She would never want to abandon her parents, nor her sister and brother. He tried to convince her otherwise, saying that even if her parents were set on staying, she could make another decision if the moment were right. She wasn't convinced, but it didn't seem to matter. There was room for disagreement in their deepening relationship.

Seated on the Cubana de Aviación jet as it soared over the Atlantic, Paquito hid his emotions of sadness, bitterness, and creeping fear. But he couldn't entirely conceal his nervousness. One of his bandmates asked him, "What's up with your hair?"

He wore his usual Afro, but he noticed something wrong when he looked into the lavatory mirror. His hair was covered with dandruff. It must be the stress, he thought. Paquito put on a straw hat that he had brought, hiding the only physical sign of what he was about to do.

Once on the ground in Madrid, Paquito went about his business as

naturally as possible in the airport. He shared a bottle of rum with Carlos
Emilio. During the six-hour wait for the flight to Scandinavia, Paquito set
down his saxophone case and carry-on bag under a table in the waiting
room. When the boarding call came, he was safely in the men's room.
When he came out, he saw only the backside of Chucho Valdés as the
pianist boarded the plane. Paquito hurried off in the other direction, picking up his bags and then slipping away.

The telephone rang in Maura Rivera's home in New York. It was her
daughter Rosario.

"*Mami*," she said, "Paquito has taken asylum in Spain."

In shock, Maura found a chair and crumpled into it. When she had
gathered her senses, Maura called a travel agent. The next day, she
boarded a plane for Madrid.

Before she arrived, Paquito had been staying at the apartment of a
Cuban doctor—the daughter of a friend in Havana—who had opened her
home to him. Now Maura arranged for a room in a guesthouse where she
could stay with Paquito. Despite the joy of being together, Maura was
acutely aware of the fact that one son still remained in Cuba. "Now we
have to get Enrique out of there," she told Paquito.

She and Paquito were awakened that night by a knock at the door.
There was a call for Maura, and she went to find out what it could be.

"*Mami*, are you standing up?" It was Rosario.

"What is it, Rosi?"

"Sit down," she said. "Enriquito is in Key West!"

Maura shouted the news to Paquito, but he was skeptical.

"If I left Enrique sitting in the living room of our house, how could he
be in Key West?" he wondered.

As it turned out, Enrique had boarded a boat at Mariel and had left the
very same day. They had defected on Mother's Day, and it was the greatest
gift Maura could ever have had.

Word of Paquito's defection spread swiftly through his neighborhood in
Marianao. It was after dark when a friend called Eneida to alert her that
members of the local Committee for the Defense of the Revolution were
headed toward the house to hold a rally.

Franco was asleep in a back room, and Eneida decided to head off trouble by confronting her accusers at the front door. She turned on all the

lights, opened the door and windows and sat in an armchair by the door to wait. More than two dozen people marched toward the house, shouting, "¡Fuera del país todos los gusanos!"

They held up protest signs, including one picturing a green worm with a photo of Paquito glued on as the head. Some marchers stuck their signs on the front of the house.

"Look, if you want to hold a condemnation rally, go do it to Paquito," Eneida told them. "But not to me here, in my house with my son!"

The crowd began to thin out as the night wore on, while Eneida kept vigil by the door. Eventually, the rally dwindled to two people. When Eneida pulled down the signs, the two went to fetch a police officer, who told Eneida she would have to come to the station for questioning. All the noise of the voices had awakened Franco, who with a grin approached the police officer and reached out to touch the gun in his holster.

"Hey, policeman," the boy said. "You're my friend."

"Look, I'm alone with my son," Eneida said. "And I can't leave him alone to go to the police station."

The officer was persuaded, and gave her a slip of paper saying she had to report to the station the next day. Nothing much came of that visit, but Eneida was soon called to a meeting at the state-run construction firm where she worked. She was fired. Next the government took away Paquito's Lada. Eneida bought a motorcycle and used it to take Franco to school. After several months, she eventually found another government job as an architect, though many of her old colleagues shunned her from that point on. Her good friends stood by her, except for one of her closest companions, Mariana, who instantly disappeared from her life. Eneida found out the reason only many years later. The state security agency had asked Mariana to act as an informant and gather details about Eneida and Paquito. When she refused, Mariana was ordered to break off her friendship, a rupture that pained Eneida for years.

While Eneida tried to get on with her life, state security agents repeatedly called her in to question her about what had led up to Paquito's defection. She always said she didn't know a thing about it.

New York City, Campus Life, a Hunger Strike

At first, Eneida tried to soften the blow for Franco.

"Your father's gone away for a while," she would tell him. Now and then, Paquito called from Spain. They were careful of what they said on the phone because they suspected the lines were tapped. Paquito heard only bits and pieces of all that Eneida had been through since he left.

After less than six months in Spain, Paquito secured a visa to join his parents in the United States and flew to New York City. It was an overwhelming feeling as the skyline came into view that day. His parents and sister were waiting as he came out of customs at Kennedy International Airport, and they hugged each other ecstatically.

Paquito moved into his parents' two-bedroom apartment in Union City. He felt overjoyed to see his father again after so many years, but Tito appeared more downcast than ever. He seemed to have aged beyond his years, perhaps because he had been apart so long from his sons and the land he loved. Tito never played the saxophone anymore. He worked stocking racks at Saks Fifth Avenue, and he complained there weren't enough opportunities for Latinos.

It hurt Paquito to see his father struggling as he did. From Paquito's perspective, reaching New York was like a breath of fresh air. He soon called Bruce Lundvall at CBS Records and said he wanted to begin recording. Bruce had promised Paquito during a visit to Spain that CBS would sign him for a solo album once he reached the United States. Paquito told Bruce it was an astounding feeling to be out of Cuba. "You don't know what it's like not to be free," Paquito told him. "For the first time in my life, I'm now free."

Paquito's joy showed in the music. In the studio, his fingers blazed across the keys. He wrote five of the eight songs on that first LP, titled *Paquito Blowin'*. He combined alto and soprano sax with Cuban rhythms, bass, and acoustic piano. The music was powerful, loaded with a soul that caught the attention of jazz fans and music critics alike.

On the liner notes, he wrote:

> Everyone has a "golden dream," and ever since I was only a child, mine was to live in the United States (New York to be precise) and build there a career as a jazz musician. After many years, this dream has been happily realized because of the generosity of my parents, who have been residents of this country for almost fifteen years, and great support and encouragement, for which I thank people such as Dizzy Gillespie, Mario Bauzá, Bruce Lundvall and David Amram.[1]

As Paquito's career took off in the United States, his music was no longer promoted in Cuba, and mentions of his name faded from the state-controlled press.

Paquito's personal struggles showed in his music. One of his first tunes recorded, "Song to My Son," captured the sadness of separation with mournful phrases on the saxophone and a dark bass line. He wrote another song for Eneida, embellishing a romantic tune with riffs he played on a flute. It was called "Monga," his affectionate nickname for her. Paquito kept in touch with her by phone and occasionally through notes delivered by friends traveling to Cuba. He missed her, though he also felt a distance growing between them.

Nancy and Fico saw each other as much as their studies allowed while they crisscrossed paths at Las Villas Central University. One of Cuba's premier colleges, it was a collection of two-story buildings just outside Santa Clara with a distinctly 1950s American architectural style. Lawns stretched between the classrooms, dotted with palms, pines, and eucalyptus trees.

Nancy enrolled in classes for her chemical engineering major: calculus, physics, general chemistry, thermodynamics, physical chemistry, balance of materials, chemical analysis, fluid flow, descriptive chemistry, descriptive geometry, linear algebra. She also took other required classes: scientific communism, economy and socialism, capitalist economy, Marxist-Leninist philosophy 1 and 2, and history of the labor movement and the revolution in Cuba.

Like other students, Nancy lived on allowances—fifteen pesos a month from the state and forty pesos a month from her father. She slept in a dormitory with a dozen other young women, some of whom she had known for years—Marisela, Ileana, Mercedes, and Odalys. When they were not studying, they chatted on their bunks or listened to pop music in English on the radio.

Nancy spent most weekends with Fico, sometimes dancing at parties to the music of the Bee Gees or ABBA. Other times they went camping in the Sierra del Escambray with friends, returning to a favorite spot by the lake at Hanabanilla Falls, where they put up tents near the water's edge, boiled wild plantains over a fire, and strummed a guitar under the stars.

At the university, Nancy's days were busy—mornings filled with classes, afternoons of lab sessions, and nights of studying. She joined a dozen other *militantes* for their Communist Youth meeting once a month, reading Fidel's speeches and discussing current affairs. Sometimes they met hurriedly before class, finishing in as little as ten minutes.

To serve the country, students were expected to volunteer for agricultural work on weekends and during part of the summer vacation. During the potato harvest, Nancy woke up early on Saturdays to catch a bus and help in the fields. She also picked guava and snapped ears of corn from their stalks. She dreaded working in the cornfields because the stalks cut her hands, but she generally did whatever was needed.

Military training also was part of the curriculum. Students were divided into squads that reported for class and held drills in an open field once a week. Nancy and others in her platoon learned to take apart their rifles, clean them, load them, and fire them. They marched in formation and practiced throwing nonexplosive hand grenades. Sometimes they stood in trenches while taking shots on a firing range.

Years later, long after she had graduated from the university, Nancy still reported for militia duty one weekend every few months. She joined women of all ages for the drills. They took to the countryside with rifles to practice defending the island against an American attack. Nancy loaded, aimed, and fired her gun with familiarity and confidence. For the most part, she was satisfied doing it all for her country, *la patria*.

In October 1981, Paquito got a call from a singer who at the last minute was looking for fill-in help. Another saxophonist hadn't shown up for a recording session on Seventh Avenue, and a sound engineer who knew of Paquito had recommended him. The soprano, Brenda Feliciano, had never heard of Paquito D'Rivera, but she decided to give him a chance.

Brenda, a Puerto Rican who had spent most of her life in New York, made her living singing jingles for commercials and working in theater. Her voice was heard in Spanish-language radio advertisements proclaiming "*¡Un fin de semana, con Michelob!*" and "*¡7-Up, qué sabor tan fascinante, una lluvia de frescura!*"

Her recording session with Paquito turned out to be the start of a long-lasting collaborative relationship. Brenda thought the bespectacled musician looked a bit like an uncle of hers. Paquito was attracted to Brenda and admired her music. He asked her to write the lyrics to a song for him. More than anything, Paquito wanted to see her again.

After a short tour filling in with Dizzy Gillespie's band, Paquito was back in New York. More and more, his thoughts drifted to Brenda.

But when they were together, Brenda could feel he was hurting inside. He had a way of walking hunched over, with his eyes to the ground. Though he often made jokes, she could feel his sadness. When they went out for dinner, Paquito's emotions sometimes overwhelmed him.

"If only Franco were here," he exclaimed to Brenda. "Oh my God, my son doesn't have any food. And look, I'm eating this!"

On Paquito's second solo album, Brenda wrote the lyrics for a song called "New York is You" that honored his close attachment to his new home. Paquito wrote an instrumental song and called it "Mariel," reflecting the tension and bitterness of the exodus.

The Mariel boatlift brought about 125,000 Cubans to the United States. Most of them ended up in Miami. They included criminals and the insane, a segment that gave the *marielitos* a bad reputation for a time. But others simply joined the workforce in Miami and blended in, making the city more predominantly Cuban.

Paquito's experiences during the exodus had given resonance to the blue notes in his music, and he decided to name that second album *Mariel*. For the cover photo, Paquito's old friend Alberto Romeu, now a studio photographer in Miami, captured an image of Paquito looking skyward, then superimposed it on an image of the sea that so many Cubans had crossed. The sea represented the distance he felt. During a 1982 interview with a journalist in Puerto Rico, Paquito paused before a window facing the sea and grew pensive.

"My only frustration is my country," he said. "It hurts me to see so much beauty lost, so much talent ruined."

When the reporter asked about his choice between his family and his career, he said: "It was terrible. A difficult price to pay. It's the choice between a mediocre, frustrated future and the possibility to be who I am, to fulfill myself. It's something I don't regret, but it tears me apart."

He smiled at times during the interview, but also added, "Those who suffer the most are those who laugh the most."[2]

Nancy was in her second year of university studies by the time Fico graduated in 1982 with his degree in electrical engineering. His next step was already decided: as part of Cuba's social service program, he went to the east to work in the small fishing town of Santa Cruz del Sur. He repaired fishing boats and maintained compressors that were used to freeze fish, lobster, and shellfish for export. After every thirty days of work, he had ten days off and returned to be with Nancy.

On December 2, 1983, Nancy and Fico married in a simple ceremony at the civil registry in Sagua la Grande. They wanted no priest, no wedding veil. Both wore jeans and T-shirts. Nancy's family watched with several close friends as the newlyweds signed the document and kissed.

Friends and family filled the Lledes family apartment for the wedding party. To buy beer, one of Fico's friends had gone to the city government and told a little lie, saying that in addition to getting married, Fico was about to leave on a military mission to Angola. The government authorized ten crates of beer, and the party lasted late into the night.

The next morning, Nancy and Fico set out for Uvero. Most cabins along the rickety dock sat empty because of the chilly December weather. The two had the beach to themselves and spent the weekend submerged in love and daydreaming about the future. Fico had two more years of work left under the program, and Nancy had two more years of university. After that, they decided, they would be together for good.

Living on the island, it was rather easy for Nancy to ignore the wars that were raging in Central America, pitting Cuban-supported troops against U.S.-backed soldiers and Contra rebels. She had seen Sandinista leader Daniel Ortega on state television reports that praised him for bringing social change to Nicaragua. But she knew little about the tens of thousands being killed in El Salvador, Guatemala, and Honduras, many of them poor *campesinos* with little allegiance to either side.

In October 1983, Nancy saw the news on TV when thousands of U.S. troops stormed Grenada. It was described as yet another imperialist move by the Americans.

U.S. Marines invaded with the support of several other Caribbean countries following the execution of the island's Marxist prime minister, Maurice Bishop, during a power struggle pitting him against radicals in his own government. Bishop, an admirer of Castro, was killed by a firing squad after soldiers retook a fort where he was holed up with supporters. When American troops landed, they faced only minimal resistance from Grenada's small army. At that time, hundreds of Cubans were on the island, including doctors, professors, a small number of military advisers, and engineers who were building an airport.

President Ronald Reagan defended the invasion as necessary to restore order and protect the lives of American medical students on the island. He said Grenada had become "a Soviet-Cuban colony, being readied as a major military bastion to export terrorism and undermine democracy."[3]

Fidel Castro called the accusations ridiculous, saying Cuba had simply been helping Grenada with civilian projects and the Americans had no right to intervene. "Imperialism is incapable of understanding that the secret of our excellent relations with the world's revolutionary countries and movements is based precisely on that respect," Castro said. He accused the Americans of wanting to "destroy the process and the example of Grenada" and questioned whether the CIA had a hand in sparking discord in the government. He said the invasion fit the mold of U.S. interventions intended to stamp out communism in places from Chile to El Salvador. "How much it has cost our nations in blood, sacrifice, misery and mourning!"

"Imperialism insists on destroying symbols, because it knows the value of symbols, of an example, of ideas. It wanted to destroy them in Grenada, it wants to destroy them in El Salvador, in Nicaragua, in Cuba. But symbols, examples, ideas cannot be destroyed, and when their enemies believe they have destroyed them, what they have done—in reality—is to multiply them."

Castro closed the speech with his forceful call to arms: "*¡Patria o Muerte! ¡Venceremos!*"[4]

Eloy and other inmates at Boniato prison had decided the only way to demonstrate their rejection of the miserable living conditions would be to hold a massive and long-running hunger strike. Eloy led the scores of inmates who began refusing meals. He was committed to demonstrating his belief that he was still a political prisoner and that he would not be broken by the system. Some inmates at the prison near Santiago also had complained of strip searches before and after family visits.[5] As days dragged on without food, Eloy felt the strength of his beliefs despite his weakening body. He and the others drank only water.

After several weeks, less than two dozen men were left. Eloy let his mind fade to blank and told himself that food no longer existed for him. He felt gnawing pain as contractions gripped his stomach, but he would not give in.

The authorities, apparently beginning to grow concerned, sent guards to fetch the hunger strikers. The men were escorted to a hospital and were given three cups of sweetened tea each day to keep them alive. After a month, the authorities stopped giving them tea. Eloy thought it was a plan to force him and the other four remaining hunger strikers to give it up. The prisoners were returned to their cellblock. Weeks passed again, and the hunger strikers' bodies shrank to little more than skeletons.

Before long, Eloy's breathing was painful. It seemed as if his heart was beating outside his body. Seeing that the hunger strikers were in danger, guards returned and took the men back to the hospital. This time the prisoners were fed a dextrose solution by intravenous drip. It was about 300 calories a day, enough to keep them alive. After another month, that treatment ended too, and the men were taken back to their dimly lit isolation cells.

When a person does not eat for such long periods, time becomes a blur and consciousness is fleeting. Eventually, Eloy knew his choice was life or death. The guards delivered a copy of a state newspaper with an editorial saying the revolution had erred in not executing Gutiérrez Menoyo when the opportunity arose. Eloy read the subtext: halt the strike or we will let you die.

Eloy was one of four who finished the hunger strike, after what he thought had been nearly five months. Another man had dropped out just a few days earlier when someone in the hospital told him that a dead man lying next to him—with only his feet exposed from under a sheet—was Eloy.

As the four began to drink water mixed with sugar, doctors came to examine them. Eloy weighed about seventy pounds—a living skeleton, but somehow alive. The next day, he had a glass of milk. Then mashed potatoes. He felt satisfied that he and his comrades had shown they wouldn't give up. Although they hadn't received any pledges from the prison administration that their treatment would improve, Eloy felt they had achieved perhaps their most important goal: they had stood up to their jailers.

In March 1984, Fidel Castro stopped in Madrid on his return from a visit to Moscow. At Barajas Airport, he and the Spanish prime minister, Felipe González, held a press conference. With reporters crowded around holding tape recorders, someone asked Fidel about Eloy Gutiérrez Menoyo. He began his answer calmly, patiently, explaining why Eloy should not be freed.

"Gutiérrez Menoyo landed in Cuba, coming from the United States. After he landed, there was combat, in which some of our comrades died," Fidel explained. "And for that reason he was sentenced."

"He also is the leader of an active counterrevolutionary group that plots acts of terrorism in our country, that tries to infiltrate armed people to carry out sabotage, to assassinate leaders of the revolution. And that organization is closely linked to the CIA. Were it not for that reason, we would have freed him a long time ago."

Fidel was speaking faster now, and he shook a finger in the air for emphasis.

"But I ask you—is it right for us to free an active boss of a terrorist organization that works with the CIA?"

Then Fidel changed course: "Nevertheless, for me Spain and President

Felipe González are more important than any other consideration, and so we don't rule out considering the possibility of a solution to that problem, which has been used demagogically to criticize Cuba and the Spanish government."

The Spanish prime minister, standing next to Fidel with his arms folded, smiled.

In a cell by himself at Boniato, Eloy heard the news through other prisoners who had met with relatives. One inmate's voice echoed through the cellblock late one night.

"¡*Oye*, Menoyo . . . *Oye*, Menoyo! In Spain they're trying to free you."

10

Cuban Dominoes, the Long Wait, Freedom

Paquito and Brenda began living together and moved into a high-rise apartment at Manhattan Plaza on Forty-second Street. Back in Cuba, Eneida adapted to the reality of their breakup. She started dating other men. But for years she and Paquito remained married on paper, agreeing that with the bond intact, it would likely be easier for Franco to leave Cuba one day to be with his father.

Paquito maintained contact with Eneida and Franco as much as possible. It could take an hour or more of dialing and redialing to get through, so the calls became sporadic. Paquito tried to give them emotional and financial support, sending letters and money with musicians who were traveling to the island. As Christmas neared, two foreigners appeared at their house in Marianao saying they had brought gifts from Paquito. Franco, who had just returned from school, was struck by the visitors' accents and the scent of perfume. The man and woman opened up their bags. They had brought photos and videos of Paquito playing with Dizzy Gillespie and appearing on TV with David Letterman. They pulled out a yellow jogging suit for Franco and another special gift: an e-flat piccolo clarinet, Franco's first. He was excited by it, and even more thrilled that his father had sent it all the way from New York. That made him want to be like his father all the more.

Paquito told Brenda he worried about what could happen if he didn't get Franco out soon. "I would lose my son," he said. So he asked her for a favor: Would she go to Cuba and help Eneida make the decision to come with Franco? She immediately accepted, believing wholeheartedly in the mission. Because the U.S. embargo prohibited traveling to Cuba under most circumstances, she flew through Canada posing as a tourist. Once in Havana, she left the tour group behind at the Capri Hotel and sneaked off to rent a car, eventually finding a late model Lada, which she steered through streets filled with 1950s American jalopies. Looking for Eneida's house, Brenda was soon lost. She returned to the hotel and called some of Paquito's friends, who helped orient her. Once she knew the route, she took it every day. She also noticed a man who seemed to be following her in a car each day—her minder, she thought.

Eneida received her graciously, and in the days they spent together Brenda urged her to take Franco and leave. Brenda assured Eneida it could work. "Do come," Brenda told her fervently. "We would help you with whatever you need to set up a new life."

As her five years in the university neared an end, Nancy wrote a thesis about "direct white sugar," a special process of making sugar without refining it. She graduated with a grade point average of 4 on a 5-point scale. Nancy was twenty-three and eager to settle into a working life. There were state jobs available in Sagua la Grande, but Fico preferred to work in the oil industry near the famous beaches of Varadero.

The industrial compound of the Empresa de Perforación y Extracción de Petroleo was located on the highway between Varadero and Cárdenas. At nearby oil fields once run by American companies, oil pumps rose and fell. The odor of sulfur emanated from the plant, and at night a blue flame rose from the tallest smokestack. That blue light could be seen from miles away in Varadero across the bay.

When both Nancy and Fico began working at the plant in August 1985, the company offered them temporary living quarters in a small wooden house in Cárdenas. They lived close enough to walk to work. Nancy was assigned to the laboratory and found the job fascinating. She worked with dense crude oil that required thorough processing because it was loaded with large amounts of dissolved heavy elements. Samples from various wells arrived at the lab, where technicians calculated the percentage of water, sulfur, and asphaltenes in the oil. Before starting in her job, Nancy had thought water and oil were easy to separate, but she soon learned that this type of oil had to be treated with chemicals to separate the water.

Shipments of crude were also coming from the Soviet Union for refining. They called the Russian oil *Romasquino*. It was combined with the heavier Cuban oil and then sent to the refinery. In the lab, workers put oil samples in beakers and determined the density. They wore gloves and white lab coats so thin that any spilled oil stained their clothes underneath.

Nancy made calculations with pencil and paper, and loaded test tubes into a centrifuge that separated oil from water and other elements. When she removed the test tubes, she lifted them to the light and saw the black crude floating atop the water.

The lab workers prepared Russian tea at break time and added a squeeze of lime to it. The label on the tea box read "*Envasado en Cuba*," but the tea itself came from Russia in bulk. A small allowance of coffee was distributed to employees, but since Nancy didn't drink coffee, she kept it and took it to her mother in Sagua la Grande.

In other jobs, Nancy knew workers often stole what they needed from their workplaces to use at home, including everything from butter to nails. Some sugar mill workers would go out on the streets selling homemade candies made with pilfered sugar. But it was different in Nancy's oil lab. The machines and industrial tools were of little use except at work, so theft was unheard of. On top of that, the lab specialists worked hard, and a friendly atmosphere prevailed. Nancy and the others often played *dominó cubano* at lunch, laying down dominoes with denominations up to the double-nine that is unique to the Cuban version of the game. Sometimes the participants became so engrossed that they didn't eat. They played in teams of two, and those who lost stood up and made way for the next pair of competitors.

All of these daily routines were set aside in November 1985 when Hurricane Kate neared Cuba's north coast with ferocious winds. Nancy and Fico rode out the storm that night in their bathroom, hearing the wind roar as it knocked out the power and tore up the roof.

Several days later, Fico went to Uvero with Nancy's mother and found that the family's cabin had been obliterated by the hurricane, along with most other homes along the shore. Her eyes filled with tears when she saw the mud and scattered debris where the cabin once stood, but Fico assured her it could be rebuilt. He started asking around about where he could find suitable wood. His boss gave him permission to salvage planks used for shipping oil drilling machinery. Fico collected boards stained with crude from oil camps damaged by the storm, and for the cabin's stilts he

Men playing *dominó cubano* in Sagua la Grande, 2001. (Ian James)

salvaged old railroad ties from a track that was being torn up. Nancy bought nails from a man who collected them, and Fico used his truck from work to carry the wood to a basement in Sagua la Grande where they stored it. Within a year, they had rebuilt the cabin in roughly the same design as before. Their neighbors in Uvero followed suit, rebuilding the row of cabins along the water with a dock connecting each front porch. The newly restored vacation retreat stood as a testament to the community's ingenuity and perseverance.

As Paquito's music gained popularity, he toured the United States and played in countries from Germany to Japan. Paquito had an unmistakable voice on the saxophone, and while playing he seemed to become one with his instrument. From mouthpiece to bell, Paquito's alto became an extension of his soul. His timing was flawless, his fingers were lightning, his tone confident. To listen to him live was like watching a world-class surfer arc across the face of a wave, maneuvering in harmony with nature.

Some fans went as far as to call him the new king of the sax. He played at the famous Blue Note with his band Havana–New York, and he hired a manager to handle all the details he didn't have time for.

He spoke heavily accented English and joked about it. In one interview for the magazine *Jazz Times* in 1983, a journalist asked, "When did you learn English?"

"I didn't yet," he retorted.[1]

As for his music, Paquito wasn't willing to compromise even if it might suit popular tastes.

"I like money," he said. "I have some purposes here to make commercial music, to make more money, but I prefer to play my music and be comfortable with myself."[2]

When his father died, Paquito's grief gave way to a desire to honor him through music. He returned to the classical music he had studied years before under his father's tutelage, appearing in chamber concerts with pianist Pablo Zinger and his group. Paquito also branched out from both classical music and his Afro-Cuban jazz. He added musical styles from Brazil, Argentina, Venezuela, and the Andes and began refining a genre that had come to be known as Latin jazz.

"All of Latin American music has the same roots, and it's very compatible with jazz," Paquito said. "We're trying to mix the multicultural thing."[3]

Even as Paquito's music evolved, he didn't forget his bandmates back in Cuba. In an interview with *Down Beat* magazine, he called Chucho Valdés "the main influence in my career" and "the best piano player I've ever heard in my life."[4]

Meanwhile, Paquito was constantly concerned with finding a way to get Franco and Eneida out of Cuba. Returning to claim them was not an option because he felt if he went back, the authorities probably would not let him leave. Thinking about his options, Paquito visited a woman in Miami who ran a market and was said to have ways of getting Cubans out of the country. For a price, she could arrange for a bribe to the right government official to get the required documents. But she warned Paquito he would have to stop talking politics in the newspapers and draw less attention to himself. So he did what she suggested and waited.

After several years of fruitless waiting, it became clear that her method was not going to work, so Paquito and Brenda began a very public campaign. Brenda wrote letters to embassies, and they both appealed to the

United Nations High Commissioner for Human Rights. Paquito even hired a public relations firm to bring the case before the public. He became furious that trying to be reunited with his son took so much effort.

Eloy hadn't watched television in years, so when a guard put a TV set outside the cellblock, he and other prisoners were mesmerized. On the screen a couple of women were talking.

One prisoner asked, "What language are they speaking?"

It was difficult to make out their words. Then Eloy responded, "They're speaking in Spanish." He and the others began to cry. After so many years without speaking to a woman, they realized they had somehow lost the ability to understand a woman's voice.[5]

The television was about to bring good news. Eloy suspected maybe that was why the guards had put it there. Through his cell bars, he watched as Spanish Prime Minister Felipe González announced that Fidel had promised freedom for a certain political prisoner by the end of the year—Eloy Gutiérrez Menoyo! It was hard to believe: somehow Castro and González had struck a deal during their meeting in November. But Eloy kept his hopes in check. Any conflict between Spain and Cuba could ruin the deal. Eloy didn't allow himself to believe it until a doctor came to give him a checkup in preparation for his release.

The day finally came. Guards opened his cell door, and as he walked out, his cellmates shouted and applauded. Eloy said his good-byes and wished them well. Then the guards drove him to a house in Santiago to wait for his departure to Spain. After a few days, he boarded a plane for Madrid. He could hardly believe it. But his happiness was tempered with sadness as he remembered the friends he left behind in prison.

"I learned that human endurance is extraordinary, greater than we imagine," Eloy told Spanish journalists on the plane. "'Endure,' I told myself, and little by little I held on."[6]

The plane touched down just before noon on December 21, 1986. Eloy felt disconnected from the outside world he hadn't seen for twenty-two years.

He was fifty-two years old. He felt weak but generally healthy. He was wearing a gray suit, a pressed white shirt, and glasses—all given to him by Cuban officials. Two representatives of the Cuban government accompanied him on the flight and rode with him in a police car across the tarmac to the airport police chief's office.

A door swung open and Eloy entered a small room where relatives and friends were waiting. Patricia's eyes instantly met his. She wept as she hugged him tightly, finally meeting the father she had known only in photographs, television footage, and letters. Their embrace seemed to go on and on.

"You have to be strong," Eloy told her, as she sniffled back tears. "You are so big," he marveled.

Before him stood a twenty-four-year-old woman he had last seen as a toddler. Examining her in amazement, he said, "You are just like I imagined you would be."

He called her Elena Patricia, even though no one had called her by both names in years. Patricia had been lobbying tenaciously to make this moment a reality, and just a day earlier someone from the Spanish foreign ministry had called her in Puerto Rico to let her know her effort had finally paid off. She came with Eloy's sister Sarita and her husband, along with a few other friends. After a round of hugs, Eloy and Patricia stepped aside to talk privately for a few minutes, and then the whole group settled onto couches in the office and carried on. Eloy and Patricia eventually drifted toward the police chief, who was seated at his desk, and thanked him for his hospitality. Then it was time to go. Others were waiting for them in the airport. Eloy and Patricia emerged from a hallway arm in arm and paused atop a staircase. Below, dozens of Cubans stood cheering and waving flags. Cameras clicked and flashed. Eloy lifted a hand and waved briskly.

Patricia's eyes began to tear up again, but her father admonished her, "Don't cry anymore. *No llores más.*"

From the top of the stairs, he spoke briefly to the crowd below, thanking the Spanish government and those who had demanded his release.

"In the dungeons and in the prisons, I could feel your solidarity despite my isolation," he said.[7]

Shouts rose from the crowd: "*¡Viva Menoyo!*" "*¡Muerte al comunismo de Fidel!*" "*¡Cuba vencerá!*"

"I'm worn out and very tired," he added, "not because of the trip but because of the emotion I feel."[8]

Outside on the street, Eloy found a dizzying world where people

Eloy talks to reporters upon his release in Spain on December 21, 1986. He is accompanied by his daughter Patricia. (AP/Wide World Photos)

seemed to move at incredible speeds. Even pedestrians crossing the street appeared to be racing. He squinted as his eyes adjusted to the bright light.

Eloy also badly needed to find a restroom. It was more than just nature calling. Inside his rectum, he carried what the prisoners called a *bala*, or a bullet, a bunch of letters rolled up like a cigar, bound with thread and covered with wax. Some of the letters that Eloy sent to his daughter had left prison with other inmates in the same way. He now had to get rid of the *bala* urgently. As soon as they arrived at their hotel, Eloy went straight to the bathroom.

"Elena Patricia, come here!" he shouted from the toilet. As she approached the doorway, his hand appeared, clutching the wet mass.

"Clean it up, clean it up," Eloy said. Surprised, Patricia hesitated, not knowing what he held. Then she took it. "*Una bala*," her father explained.

She wiped it off, scraped off the wax, and together they unrolled the papers inside. It held about thirty letters written on thin paper, plus a passport-size photograph of a prisoner, Ernesto Díaz González, who was like a son to Eloy.

Later that day, Eloy sat in front of a Christmas tree in the home of family friends talking to a reporter from the newspaper *El País*. Patricia watched her father intently, studying his features as he spoke. Perched on his nose were the same black-rimmed glasses he had worn for years.

"After all these years, how has your ideology changed? What is the revolution for you?" the reporter asked.

"My ideas haven't changed," Eloy said. "I don't support a revolution when it's synonymous with tyranny, and I don't think one thing has anything to do with the other. If I thought that way, I would no longer be a revolutionary. A revolution doesn't consist of taking over power to enjoy it, nor of displacing a privileged class to put in place another privileged class. When a revolutionary accepts a dictatorship, he becomes an enemy of the proletariat."

Eloy smoked a cigarette and sipped a Coca-Cola.

"If I had known Castro better, I would have faced him much sooner," he added. "I have never given up my ideals; I don't and I won't."[9]

Eloy wasn't used to seeing walls decorated with photographs and paintings. It seemed to him that the walls were loaded down, that all of it was unnecessary. He went to bed exhausted, but he found it was difficult to sleep in a normal bed instead of his prison cot.

Adapting took time. When Eloy showered in the hotel, he scalded his back because he wasn't accustomed to the shower handle that had to be turned to the right or left to adjust the temperature. Among the toiletries Patricia brought for her father was "Dry Look" hairspray. He sprayed it under his arms, thinking it was deodorant.

Eloy had to reacquaint himself with using a knife, fork, and spoon at mealtime. At first, when served a soup, he simply lifted the bowl to his lips and drank.

Nevertheless, he hadn't lost his touch as an orator. Eloy spoke with indignation about conditions in Cuban prisons, where he recalled abuse and solitary confinement and said he was treated "like an animal."

"I don't think there is any prisoner in Cuba whose body hasn't been beaten," he told journalists the day after his arrival.

He was scathing in his criticism of Fidel Castro.

"The Cuban people have learned to put on a mask and clap constantly, and amid the endless noise they are unable to think. They have become like sheep cheering their leader," he said bitterly. "He doesn't notice that the clapping is not real."[10]

"The Cuban revolution is condemned to total failure because it is a revolution against the people and against the interests of the proletariat and, above all, because from a seed planted in blood and ashes only a small and crooked tree with bitter roots can grow."

Despite Eloy's joy at being free and seeing his daughter again, he felt a lingering sadness. Patricia took him to a restaurant expecting to treat him to whatever he wanted. But he looked at the menu and remained silent, unable to order.

"What's wrong?" she asked.

He paused, then answered: "Don't you understand that for twenty-two years I haven't been able to choose anything? All of a sudden you bring me to a place where I can choose absolutely whatever I want, but all of my brothers in prison are eating whatever they're being given. And if there is macaroni now, they'll be eating macaroni for the whole month straight. And here, you're asking me to choose between Jesus, Holy Mary, and Joseph—the appetizer, dessert, everything. I can't."

It took months for Eloy to adjust.

He had missed most of the major events in his daughter's life, but he was just in time for her wedding. The ceremony was held in a banquet hall in San Juan, Puerto Rico, where Patricia lived. Fifty extra seats had to be added for people who hadn't been invited but came especially to see Eloy. When he escorted the bride into the hall, the sight of them together brought people to their feet. Their applause hung in the air for several minutes. Some even shouted, "*¡Viva Cuba Libre!*"

Three weeks later, in March 1987, Eloy visited Miami for the first time since he had set out on his ill-fated mission to Cuba. Leaders of Alpha 66 organized a rally to welcome him, and he reluctantly agreed to go.

He strode into the stadium at Tropical Park to wild applause, and raised his fists triumphantly as a crowd of more than 3,000 people applauded. Some held Cuban flags and chanted, "*¡Viva Menoyo!*" Stepping onto a stage on the baseball field, Eloy was greeted by the mayors of Miami, Miami Beach, and the predominantly Cuban suburb of Hialeah.

They presented him with proclamations praising his release, and Eloy stepped to the microphone to make a speech.

"The Cuban revolution is fractured," he said. "We must get together. We must never forget that we are brothers in making Cuba free."[11]

Some were taken aback when he began to talk about forgiveness and making peace. Others listened intently. Quoting José Martí, Eloy declared: "For my enemies, I cultivate a white rose."[12]

11

Weariness, a Reunion, Speaking Out

After their first year working for the oil company, Nancy and Fico were assigned a two-bedroom apartment in a plain, Soviet-style building in Cárdenas. Most of the workers lived in the same concrete complex, and their employer covered a portion of the rent.

They got up early every day to catch a company bus to work, and they took the same bus back in the evening. On her way home, Nancy often stopped off at the state grocery store where she was registered. The bodega was a dimly lit counter that offered few choices. She carried her *libreta*, the government booklet entitling her to fixed amounts of rice, bread, sugar, and other foods each month. A shopkeeper handed out whatever had arrived that day, from fish to eggs, to the people lined up. Because items were given out according to *libreta* number, Nancy had to go by the market frequently to see if it was her turn. Each day, those within a certain range of *libreta* numbers would receive their allotments. The lines were particularly long at the beginning and end of the month, or when meat was available. Sometimes the market closed while Nancy was still in line. When she did come home with food, it was often just enough for her and Fico to get by for a couple of days. Because they didn't drink coffee or smoke cigarettes, Nancy bartered her ration to others in exchange for more food. The market provided milk only to families with children, so Nancy obtained hers through a man who had several cows and sold the milk.

Some of her most memorable meals came when she and Fico would spend a weekend spearfishing in Varadero. They brought masks, fins, and a homemade spear gun rigged with a rubber cord. They were breaking the law whenever they did it because the government prohibited spearfishing to protect stocks of fish that could be sold to tourists or for export. But Nancy and Fico didn't think twice when they waded in along the white sand beaches. They usually swam offshore near a rocky point, and Fico took aim at *pargo, pez perro,* and *picuda* while Nancy strung the speared fish from a small buoy towed behind them. Looking to the bottom, they saw soft corals swaying with the ocean atop spines of rock that jutted from the sandy seafloor. In the silence of this liquid world, Nancy felt entirely at peace.

Even though she rarely showed it, there were personal stresses in Nancy's life. She badly wanted to have a baby but had been unable to get pregnant after more than four years of trying. In 1988, she decided to travel to Havana for medical tests to find out why. Just as she began to undergo those tests, the surprise came: she was pregnant. Nancy felt as if her yearning for a baby had somehow unlocked a physiological door in her.

As her belly grew, she dreamed of what lay ahead. Nothing could have been more important to her. She and Fico decided to name their daughter Clara Celia.

Months later, Nancy was in a hospital bed having contractions when a nurse put a sensor to her abdomen to check the heartbeat. There was none. The baby was dead.

It seemed impossible, but as the sadness of the truth came over her, Nancy had to continue with the birth. The baby emerged still, silent. She had died choked by her umbilical cord, perhaps just a day or two earlier. Instead of comforting Nancy, doctors in the maternity ward were accusatory. One stood at her bed and asked why she had come to the hospital instead of just staying in Cárdenas. By bringing the baby to die in their hospital, he said, she was bringing down their rate of successful births. Nancy was numb with grief. Her mother came to the hospital. She saw the baby girl who had just died—her fully formed body, her dark hair. She looked without speaking and without crying. Nancy didn't cry then either, but the pain washed over her for months. She didn't feel up to talking to anyone, not even her friends.

A burden of rigid goals and less-than-perfect conditions at times weighed on Cuba's health care system, which regularly won praise internationally for its well-trained doctors and free, universal care. Fidel Castro had sought to make medical care one of the pillars of his socialist system, and the number of practicing doctors grew sharply in the 1970s, 1980s, and 1990s, outpacing population growth. The island's medical schools trained not only Cubans but also students from various other countries. Cuba's doctors were paid a pittance in comparison to their colleagues elsewhere, and state hospitals frequently lacked needed supplies, particularly in the 1990s after the fall of the Soviet Union and the disappearance of its large subsidies. But Cuba made generous use of its doctors' services even in financially difficult times, sending volunteers to treat patients for free in dozens of receptive countries across the world. Some Cubans called it a political ploy, while others said the humanitarian missions were an indisputable achievement of socialism.

As his fame grew, Paquito sometimes autographed record sleeves with the words "Love and Swing." In 1988, he called his new album *Celebration*, writing in the liner notes that the songs were a celebration of his recently granted U.S. citizenship. "I am proud now to be an official part of this country, and I am proud to call it my home."[1]

At the same time, Paquito was growing increasingly furious as he waited for Cuba to grant exit visas for Franco and Eneida.

A U.N. human rights commission visited the island in 1988 to evaluate the human rights situation, and Eneida was one of the first people on a list called to testify. She appeared in a hotel conference room, seated at one end of a long table while the commission president sat at the other, flanked by delegation members. Eneida told them the government had refused to let her and her son leave the island to be with her husband, and was therefore essentially holding them captive. The panel's response was mixed, with some members receptive and others appearing defensive of the Cuban government. Eneida left the meeting with no clear answers about her fate.

As the end of the year approached, Paquito decided to write an open letter to Fidel Castro to demand the release of Eneida and Franco. It was published in *Diario Las Americas* on December 21, 1988.

Señor Presidente:
     This letter is my public complaint against the Cuban government for the abuse and violations of human rights committed systematically against

members of my family, held on the island after being denied permission to leave on numerous occasions.

First of all, I should tell you that I am not addressing you as a compatriot, since it is well known that Cuban citizenship is worth very little to thousands of us born in the land of Martí who don't agree with the totalitarian rules you imposed 30 years ago.

Much less will I appeal to your sensitivity as a father or human being. No one who represents such a brutal, arbitrary and inhuman government and system as yours could be moved by anything except Marxist manuals or Che Guevara's death in combat.   ·

No, *señor presidente*, I completely refuse to share my nationality with characters so sinister as Raúl Castro or Ramiro Valdés . . . and this letter that you are receiving today is a formal complaint and protest against your government. And as the U.S. citizen that I am, I demand the immediate liberation of my son Franco and his mother Eneida, held on the island against their will, and our right to freely reunite in this country.[2]

Less than two weeks after the letter was published, the Cuban government finally sent word that Eneida and Franco would fly to Miami in three days—on January 3, 1989. The news had come when Paquito least expected it, while on tour in Japan. He quickly caught a flight back, buying a T-shirt for his son at a souvenir shop in the Tokyo airport. He and Brenda were already waiting at the Miami airport by midnight, though the flight wasn't scheduled to arrive until 3 a.m.[3]

Sitting in the terminal and nervous beyond words, Paquito lit a cigarette while Brenda put an arm around him. He straightened his Panama hat. Eight years had passed since Paquito had seen Franco. He was thirteen now. How would it be to see his son after such a long time?

The plane landed thirty minutes late, and it took two more hours for the passengers to clear immigration and customs before they finally began filing out.

"Your family is on the plane! They're coming!" called out one Cuban who recognized Paquito. He grinned back nervously. Minutes passed. Then suddenly his son strode through the doors. Franco rushed to his father's open arms.

"*¡Mi hijo! ¡Mi hijo!*" Paquito cried. "I thought I'd never see you again!"[4]

A photographer captured the moment as Paquito held Franco tightly, his eyes closed and relief sweeping across his face.

Paquito is reunited with his son Franco in Miami, January 1989. (Acey Harper/
People)

As soon as Eloy arrived in Miami, a wealthy Cuban who had been among
his rebels in the Escambray offered his former chief a house in the sub-
urbs, giving him a key and saying, "You don't have to rent a house."

Located at the end of a quiet cul-de-sac, the house was secluded and
comfortable. Eloy settled in quickly, meeting regularly with old comrades
and making new acquaintances as well. He still spoke forcefully against
Castro, saying the country needed major changes. But unlike years before,
he no longer talked of armed insurrection. He felt the country needed a
safer, peaceful transition.

At one party, Eloy met his old friend Rafael Huguet, who had come to
visit him in prison nearly a decade earlier. Rafael presented Eloy to his
niece Gladys Teresa Martínez, knowing they had met long ago in Havana
when she was just a toddler.

"I bet you don't recognize her," Rafael said.

"Yeah, that's your niece!" Eloy said. "You can never forget those eyes."
All those years he had remembered her piercing green eyes.

Gladys didn't remember Eloy at all, but her family later told her that as
a young girl she had a cloth doll she called Menoyito after the famous

rebel who had visited her house. Gladys had left Cuba when she was three and moved to Mexico with her family. As a young woman, she came to the United States. Of her childhood in Cuba, she had only a faint memory of passing through a tunnel in the Havana neighborhood of Miramar. That was all. And part of what made Eloy attractive to Gladys was his deep connection to the land she had left behind and knew so little about. He was fifty-four and she was thirty-two.

They quickly began dating and married in early 1989. Their first son, Carlos, was born five days before Christmas that year. Eloy named him in honor of his father and his brother—a connection to Cuba for a boy who would have a thoroughly American childhood.

A world away from the shopping malls and busy highways of Miami, Nancy and Fico spent their days with few time pressures and little concern about material wealth. One day in the lab, Nancy was washing oil off her hands when her gold engagement ring slipped off and disappeared down the drain. She felt sorry, but she wasn't particularly worried about how much the ring had cost. What mattered most was its sentimental value.

Nights at home, Nancy often had time to watch popular Brazilian television dramas. On the weekends she frequently left Cárdenas with Fico, squeezing onto a crowded bus or hitchhiking to visit her family in Sagua la Grande. Hitching rides was common, with many people standing along the highway *haciendo botella*, or "making a bottle," with hand and thumb outstretched. No matter how they traveled, the trip could be unpredictable—with a broken-down bus or a lengthy wait for a ride. Sometimes Nancy and Fico were lucky and made it in about two hours. Other times, the journey home seemed to take forever.

In some ways, Sagua la Grande was a town frozen in time. People paused to chat on streets lined with two-story buildings that had remained unchanged for decades. But Nancy's mother was quick to point out that much had changed over the years. She had retired from the phone company, and Benjamín had retired from an office job with the police. Within their lifetimes, Sagua's central plaza had gone from being a place where blacks were forbidden to walk among whites to a place where all shades mingled. Nancy's mother felt the revolution had righted the town's wrongs. She remembered years ago seeing poor children without shoes playing in the dirt on the outskirts of town. Now they had shoes, she pointed out, and free schooling.

Fico, on the other hand, didn't believe the communist system offered him or Nancy much of a future. At home in Cárdenas, he tuned in to Miami radio stations, keeping the volume low so the neighbors wouldn't hear. One man in a nearby building had been arrested for shouting "Down with Fidel!" from his balcony after having too many drinks. So Fico knew he had to be discreet.

Because it was expected of them, he and Nancy often went downstairs in the evenings for meetings of the neighborhood Committee for the Defense of the Revolution. Together they analyzed Fidel's latest speeches, discussed neighborhood business, and drew up schedules of when each person would take a shift keeping vigil.

At the end of each meeting, they recited: "*¡Viva la Revolución! ¡Viva el Socialismo! ¡Viva Fidel!* Fatherland or Death! We will prevail!"

These were just hollow words for Fico. He was growing weary of a system that he felt denied people their freedom. When police questioned Fico for sitting on a beach in Varadero, he was furious. Wasn't it his beach, too? Or was it just for the foreign tourists? What about the Cubans?

The Berlin Wall had fallen, but in Cuba there would be no perestroika, Fico said. Things wouldn't change. Fico felt frustrated by the lack of options, by the fact that there were only two channels to choose from on television. More and more, Fico's mouth got him into arguments. In Communist Party meetings and gatherings at work, he questioned the purposes of government-sanctioned organizations like the newly created Rapid Response Brigades, civilian groups that were created to help keep order but were also known to break up protests by force. Fico said these sorts of groups existed for the sole purpose of controlling the population—a view that prompted strong rebuttals from his coworkers. Fico's willingness to speak his mind made Nancy so afraid of what might happen that she sometimes cried at night.

"What are you trying to do?" she scolded him. "Shut up, please shut up. Because no matter what, you aren't going to solve anything."

When Fico decided he had to leave Cuba, he kept his decision to himself at first. He lay awake in bed at night, thinking and planning. When he finally told Nancy, she was shocked.

"But you're going to go away and leave me?" she asked.

"No, I'm not going to *leave* you. As a last resort, I'd go and you'd stay—because you *want* to stay, but it's not that I'm going away and leaving you behind."

Fico didn't act on his plan right away, but Nancy knew that if he decided to go through with it, she could do nothing to hold him back.

When reporters asked Eloy his thoughts on Fidel Castro, his words tended to be harsh. He once declared: "Fidel is sick, a sadist, a man with a true liking for deception."[5] In another interview, Eloy called him "Nazi to the core."[6]

In Cuba, meanwhile, some spoke out against Eloy. He was the subject of a critical book, *I Was Never a Traitor: Portrait of a Fraud*, by Roberto Orihuela, including accounts from people who accused Eloy of receiving money from the CIA and who claimed his rebel group was infiltrated by the U.S. spy agency from the beginning.[7] Eloy called the accusations stupidities and insisted that he had never received CIA support.

At the same time, he clashed with many Cuban exile leaders in Miami, fiercely disagreeing with their hard-line positions. Eloy thought the embargo had been a dismal failure and that the U.S. government needed to rethink its policy. He also thought change wouldn't come from outside Cuba, but from within. He mulled over the need for a new approach while administering the financially troubled magazine *Ahora*, a project in which he had become involved through a group of friends. When the magazine eventually folded, Eloy turned his attention to politics. He knew his ideas would not find favor with most conservative exile groups, but that didn't stop him. In fact, the opposition he anticipated made him want to get involved all the more. He wanted to combat intolerance in Miami, and he wanted to give the world another image of Cuban exiles. With many of his closest confidants, Eloy formed a group called Cambio Cubano, or Cuban Change.

With George H. W. Bush leaving office and Bill Clinton just sworn in as president, it seemed the right time for a different approach. Eloy announced the founding of his group at a news conference in Washington. Soon after, in March 1993, he submitted an advertisement to Miami newspapers laying out the group's manifesto:

Our purpose is to contribute to the restoration and reunification of the Cuban nation. We wish to assist in peacefully resolving the deep tragedy that has brought us confusion, violence and disharmony, and which has divided the great national family for more than three decades.

Our country could be facing extremely dangerous times. The possibility of a bloody outcome that would unleash factional hatred cannot be ruled out. . . . However, this foreseeable danger may bring with it a hope-inspiring challenge: it is also the opportunity for all factions, acting with good sense and judgment, to find a way to end this bitter period of social tension and fratricidal ideological debate.

Cubans, don't let others speak for you. Think. Don't let ideas be eradicated. In the face of passion, rage and vociferous demagoguery, use your intelligence and remember the teachings of José Martí. Do not tolerate pressure or censorship against you in a free country. Express yourself. The time for change has come.

Cuban Change promotes a peaceful transition from the current Cuban government to a new pluralistic entity that is legitimized by consensus as well as by its tolerance for minorities.

The document listed several principles: the U.S. trade embargo could be used as a "negotiating tool" and could be narrowed until it is lifted; cultural and other exchanges with Cuba are positive; and Cuban exiles should have the right to freely travel to the island. It stated, "A Cuban who travels to Cuba is not a traitor and indeed may be an ambassador for our cause, the cause of freedom."

Near its end, the statement included an open message directed to Fidel Castro:

With the end of the Cold War and the collapse of the Soviet bloc, today more than ever your leadership of the government shall be subjected to scrutiny by new generations. Your eroded leadership now faces its gravest hour, and the country will, sooner or later, be on the verge of desperation and bankruptcy. We exhort you to join in our deliberations and assume a historic role in the task of reconciliation.

From the opposition we send you, not a slogan or demand, but a sincere and specific invitation to an open discussion, without recriminations, for the purpose of dismantling or bringing new flexibility to the structures that limit or prevent change on the island.

Your adversaries invite you to seek Cuban solutions, in an open and sincere discussion. Not to point out the guilty or the innocent, but for the simple—and at the same time magnificent—task of being true Cubans. To open up the jails, borders, mouths and hearts. To see a new Republic born. This is an appeal to your intelligence and your concern for your role in history. It is time to end the longest and most traumatic period of our intransigence. It is time to say: the war is over.

Eloy's break with the entrenched, hard-line positions of most exile groups stunned Miami's Cuban-American establishment. Some said Eloy must have gone mad. Others said he seemed to be speaking for the Cuban government. That was when he began to receive death threats in the mail.

12

Boat People

Eloy's insistence on trying to sit down and talk with Fidel Castro was what most infuriated and perplexed the Cuban exile establishment in Miami. After so many years, many asked what good talking would do. When word got out that Eloy had invested in a small business that manufactured glass souvenirs, a quiet boycott forced the business to go under. But Eloy persisted in speaking out.

"Twenty-two years in prison forces you to meditate. Those of us who have made war know what war is," he told one reporter. "If you want Fidel Castro's head, is it worth the heads of thousands of Cubans?"[1]

When insults against him became common on Miami radio shows, Eloy responded by writing a letter "to the exile community" that was published in the *Miami Herald*.

> I have been called a traitor. Once, when my son heard that accusation on the radio, he looked up to ask me if it was true. Carlos Alberto is barely 4 years old. When we play cops-and-robbers, I let him approach me stealthily and pounce on my back. Then, invariably, I accuse him of being a traitor, and he is much amused.
>
> But I'm not so amused. Not when those who call me traitor lack any reason to do so. Not when it is done by adults who should assume responsibility for their deeds and their words.
>
> Since March 13, when we published the document *For Cuba, For Change*, announcing Cambio Cubano's blueprint for a peaceful transition, some Miami politicians and radio commentators have been doing a hatchet job.
>
> I want to prevent a civil war in Cuba, and I thought (naively, I admit) that I could count on all those who "lead" the exile community. Some time

ago, when Fidel Castro predicted an apocalyptic finale to the Cuban conflict, those leaders were horrified. However, with their extremist words and
stances, they push the Cuban people to the wall and wait breathlessly for a
violent denouement.

Even under the tightest possible embargo and without significant
changes in U.S. policy toward the island, Fidel Castro could shrewdly man-
age to cling to power.

The whole world dialogues. There was dialogue in El Salvador, and now
Israel talks with the Palestine Liberation Organization. Political adversaries
of every kind face each other across a table.

The delicate accord that we seek with Havana attempts to end a family
schism lasting three decades.[2]

One of the stories that most inspired Paquito was that of Orestes Lorenzo,
a Cuban Air Force pilot who on March 20, 1991, soared away from Cuba
in a MiG-23 jet and landed at a naval air station outside Key West. After
his defection, Lorenzo began a letter-writing campaign demanding that
the Cuban government allow his wife, Vicky, and their two young sons to
join him. Cuba responded that Lorenzo was a traitor and couldn't expect
to be given priority over other exit visa applicants. After nearly two years
of waiting, he decided to try another approach. He flew back across the
Florida Straits in a Cessna on December 19, 1992, and plucked his wife
and two sons from a coastal highway where they had secretly arranged to
meet. When he arrived back in Florida, he declared: "My family, they are
free now."[3]

Touched by that act of heroism, Paquito wrote a gleeful freedom song
and called it "Lorenzo's Wings."

In his own life, Paquito was happy to be getting reacquainted with his
son. Franco lived nearby with his mother, and he finally was reestablishing
a connection with the father who for years had been just a voice on the
telephone. In Cuba, Franco sometimes heard people call Paquito a traitor.
Now he began to know the real man—the hard worker, the clown, the
virtuoso.

Just months after Franco arrived, Paquito recorded an album filled with
bright, upbeat music titled Tico Tico. He played alto and tenor saxophone
and clarinet, and the music ranged from Venezuelan waltzes to the ener-
getic title song. He recorded "Song for Maura" with birdsong and blue

notes seeming to recall years of separation. His saxophone spoke with energy, speed, and force in one of his masterpieces, "To Brenda With Love."

Paquito decided to quit smoking. His life was active, and he didn't want to compromise it. Sometimes he recorded more than one album a year. He spent less time rehearsing and poured more energy into composing, arranging, and performing on tour. He traveled first class and always carried his instrument case aboard the plane with him. He took naps before shows to calm his mind and gather strength for his performances.

Paquito still showed his playful side during concerts, holding his clarinet to one eye like a spyglass and sweeping it across the audience. When friends visited, they fed one of Paquito's boyish hobbies by bringing him small toy cars, mainly Volkswagen Beetles.

But he also had a serious side. Paquito could be brutally honest and didn't hesitate to mix his politics with his music, sometimes denouncing Fidel Castro at public events. When word got out that Americans favoring improved relations with Cuba were planning a rally at Manhattan's Javits Center, Paquito was disgusted and began to help mobilize a massive counterdemonstration. About 10,000 anti-Castro demonstrators marched from Times Square to the convention center, chanting, "Cuba sí, Castro no!" A line of police officers on foot and horseback kept them apart from others who were arriving for the pro-Castro rally. Paquito stood bundled up in the cold with marchers who had come from as far away as Miami and Spain. Some carried signs with slogans like "Don't support criminals in Cuba."[4]

Paquito's views largely matched those of the Cuban exile establishment in Miami. He firmly believed in the U.S. embargo and said there should be no attempt to reestablish relations with Cuba until Castro's demise. But there was a sinister vein among some exiles that infuriated Paquito. It had to do with race. In contrast to Cuba, where blacks were a majority, Cuban Miami was largely white, including many from the upper class who had fled the island at the first hint of a turn toward communism. Some of them still held on to their old prejudices.

Paquito was particularly offended by the comments of one old man who spoke on a call-in radio show in Miami. Paquito had been driving during a visit to Florida when he heard the show, and the comments made him so angry that he wrote a newspaper column about it. He said the old man spoke of the "difficulties we would have to rebuild our homeland upon the fall of the communist regime, basically due to the demographic explosion reflecting 80-something percent of blacks and *mestizos*, in contrast to the 80-something percent of 'pure' whites who populated the island before 1959."

Paquito couldn't believe it when the man went on to say it was shameful that in Cuba nowadays "the white girls go around brazenly with any black." Paquito said it was incredible that there were still people with such hatred:

> How quickly he forgot (or never learned of) such notable men and women as Juan Gualberto Gómez, Claudio Brindis de Salas, Antonio and José Maceo, Amadeo Roldán, Quintín Banderas, Wifredo Lam, Celia Cruz, Mariana Grajales, Guillermo Cabrera Infante and so many others who could have been the honorable ancestors of *algún que otro negrito* who goes around brazenly with a white girl in Havana, New York, Paris or Miami.
>
> This disagreeable incident brings to my memory a comment that I found in a publication in Miami, in which an individual as knowledgeable in the art of sounds as I am in marsupial gynecology categorically defines Cuban music as "Spanish with light Afroid touches."
>
> People, enough already with being "crazy goats."

Paquito said the music of the Caribbean, Brazil and the United States "exists simply and plainly by the work and grace of blacks." He wrote: "Let's give thanks to God and the 'good-for-nothings' for having brought slaves from Africa. If they had been brought from Poland we would have been quite bored dancing polkas and mazurkas."

Paquito warned that racism "only serves to feed the Marxist demagoguery, confuse and terrify those who still live on the island, divide exiles and separate us even further from African Americans, Puerto Ricans, Jews and the other communities of immigrants who form this marvelous country."[5]

Back in Cuba, people were adapting to rapid economic changes. With the collapse of Soviet communism, the island was forced to make do without its largest trading partner. Aid dwindled, and the economy rapidly contracted. Fidel Castro proclaimed this new and difficult time the *Periodo Especial*. In 1992, the National Assembly approved constitutional changes declaring nationalism a guiding principle instead of Marxist-Leninism,

calling the state secular instead of atheist and recognizing multiple categories of property instead of just state-owned.[6]

The government legalized the use of the U.S. dollar in 1993, seeking to
draw in more hard currency and prop up the economy. Before then,
Cubans had faced possible prison sentences just for possessing dollars. The
shift essentially recognized that the dollar was already being used on the
black market, and in the years that followed, access to dollars would begin
to define Cuba's haves and have-nots. Those with relatives in Miami or
with other ways of obtaining dollars could count on the goods that only
dollars could buy, while other people were often out of luck.

The withering of trade with the Soviet bloc meant Cubans had to adapt
to tighter restrictions. Meat and many other foods grew scarce in markets.
Without Russian gasoline, fewer buses were running. Blackouts plunged
entire towns into darkness.

In their jobs as engineers, Nancy earned 265 pesos a month and Fico
earned 325—a combined amount worth just several U.S. dollars at the
time. Their pay was above average, but still they spent most of it buying
foods that were rarely distributed through *libreta* rations, such as pork,
fish, or beef.

After eight years at the oil company, they were growing restless and
were ready for a change. They applied to a business administration training program to work in tourism. Applicants had to speak at least one foreign language and had to have some management experience. Nancy fit
the profile in part because she had studied English in night school, hoping
to use it someday to travel overseas.

The entrance exams also included an interview with three psychologists
to judge intelligence, personality, and temperament. One of them asked
Fico what type of movies he liked. He said films with social or historical
themes that didn't just entertain but left him with something deeper.
"And is your sexual life satisfactory?" "What do you think about the Second World War?"

"Do you like art?" Yes. "Which artists do you like?" Van Gogh,
Raphael, Goya, Dalí, Miró. "Why?" And on it went.

More than 200 people applied to the program, and the competition was
stiff. Nancy and Fico were among the twenty-seven accepted. They began
their studies in April 1992, taking classes ranging from strategic marketing
to international relations and sales.

Fico was quietly investigating ways he could leave for Miami, but he kept those thoughts to himself.

For the time being, he and Nancy were glad to be saving money by eating for free at a cafeteria with the rest of the trainees. They were beneficiaries of a new national emphasis on tourism that came as the island's sugar industry was slowly fading.

The two began working as trainees in some of the older hotels in Varadero. Nancy made beds, mixed drinks, and helped in the kitchen. The work seemed a bit repetitive, but she was determined to give it a try. New hotels were rising along the white-sand strip, and tourists from Canada, Germany, Italy, France, and Spain browsed through gift shops buying cigars and Che Guevara T-shirts. Fico went to work at the Marina Acua on the peninsula's bay side. Nancy started at the front desk of the Hotel Internacional. The four-story hotel was one of the oldest in Varadero and dated to before the revolution. Flags flew beside royal palms out front, and on the beach tourists lounged under palm-thatched parasols.

After graduating from the trainee program, Nancy and Fico stayed on as permanent employees, earning the same modest salaries they had as engineers. But Nancy was beginning to grow bored with the work, and Fico felt even more strongly about it. He didn't want to waste more years serving tourists and working for a system he didn't believe in. If he grew comfortable in this job, he thought, he might never leave. He wanted more control over his own destiny, and he began to daydream more than ever about ways to arrange a boat trip to leave Cuba.

A bad case of conjunctivitis provided the excuse Fico needed to get out of work. A certain medicine that he was taking had further irritated his eyes, so he requested a leave of absence with a doctor's note. Nancy joined him. She was glad to take the time off. They left their dormitory and set out for Sagua la Grande to stay with her parents.

Years later, Nancy recalled those times and said she would never have considered leaving if it weren't for Fico's constant prodding. The idea of abandoning her family was painful. But as it became clear that Fico was set on leaving, she decided she had no choice. Nancy knew Fico was asking around about how to leave by boat, and she decided she would try too. Though they spoke of their plans only in private, their secret didn't last long. A friend in whom Fico had confided reported him and Nancy to the *Seguridad del Estado*, the state security police, saying they intended to defect.

Before long, two agents were knocking at the door of the apartment. They told Benjamín they wanted to question his daughter and son-in-law about a plot to smuggle Cubans out of the country. Nancy's parents hadn't heard a word about it and were shocked. The agents left with Nancy and Fico in their car and took them to a cell where they were questioned for two days about what they had been planning and who was organizing their trip. When the agents finished and let them go, Nancy was sure she had no future in Cuba and would not be welcome back at work. Marked as a counterrevolutionary, she decided then that she really had to leave.

The situation for those trying to abandon the island was growing tense. At about 3 a.m. on July 13, 1994, dozens of people boarded a tugboat, the *13 de Marzo*, and set off for Florida. They were soon intercepted off Havana by three other tugboats, which trained high-pressure hoses on the fleeing boat, spraying the deck and blowing out windows. Witnesses later said the powerful streams of water swept some passengers off the deck[7] and pulled children from their mothers' arms.[8] They said the pursuing vessels rammed into the tugboat. It took on water and sank, pulling down dozens of people with it.

Though the Cuban government put the death toll at thirty-two, later news accounts in Miami reported forty-one deaths, a number of them children. The sinking became a political symbol for Castro's opponents, who said it showed his government would do just about anything to stop people from leaving. The Cuban government denied responsibility, saying it was an unfortunate accident caused by an unintended collision and brought on by people who recklessly stole a leaky tugboat that should never have left the Havana harbor.[9]

Cubans fed up with the situation continued trying to leave during the summer of 1994. After a series of ferry hijackings, riots broke out along the waterfront in Havana. Crowds of people who had come to the port in hopes of finding a departing boat resisted when police ordered them to leave the area. Some smashed windows and looted stores. Hundreds of protesters threw rocks at police, injuring several of them.[10] Police fired shots into the air. Hundreds of protesters marched down one main street chanting, "*¡Libertad! ¡Libertad!*"[11]

The violence broke out on a Friday afternoon, and thousands of pro-government workers rushed into the streets carrying metal pipes, clubs, and chains to challenge the rioters.[12] People soon dispersed, but thousands of government supporters remained in the streets and milled around Fidel chanting his name when he arrived to tour the sealed-off waterfront.

The violence angered Castro, who blamed "delinquents"[13] and threatened to open the borders to any Cubans who wanted to leave if the United States continued to welcome them with offers of political asylum. Unless the United States stops encouraging people to take to the sea, Castro said, "we will stop blocking the departure of those who want to leave the country."

"We cannot continue to guard the coasts of the United States," he said.[14]

Fico saw his chance and began making arrangements to leave on a makeshift raft of wood and tires. Nancy was prepared to go with him, but in this case no women or children were allowed. The men organizing the trip felt it would be too risky.

The day Fico left Sagua la Grande, he lifted his backpack and suddenly announced to Nancy's mother, "*Vieja, me voy.*"

Nancy told her mother about his plan. "Don't worry, you'll see that he'll be right back here in a little while," Nancy told her. She thought, or at least allowed herself to believe, that Fico's plan would fail again. But this time the days passed with no sign of him, as he and nine other men rolled along through the swells to the hum of an outboard motor.

The weather was turning rough. Nancy wasn't religious, but she prayed to God the ocean would spare him.

In the countryside, tractors lay idle, their tires missing. People had taken them to make more rafts. Nancy planned to follow Fico. She became more resolute when Fico's father called from Miami to let her know her husband had been safely picked up by an American ship and taken to the U.S. naval base at Guantánamo Bay. She didn't know all the details of Fico's journey. As it turned out, he and the other men were rescued just in time, after seven days at sea. In order to stay afloat during a storm, they had cut through the wooden supports that held the heavy outboard motor and let it sink into the sea. They continued on paddling the raft for days until

Cubans leave in a makeshift wooden boat in August 1994. (AP/Wide World Photos—José Goitia)

they were picked up by a U.S. Navy ship—sore, hungry, sunburned, and exhausted.

Nancy soon arranged to leave on a homemade boat. She found her group of *balseros* through the mother of a young man who had left with Fico. The group had welded together enough sheet metal to make the boat's hull and had mounted on it an engine from a 1956 Chevrolet. They only needed a car battery to make it run.

Nancy put up the money for the battery—thirty U.S. dollars. It was part of Nancy's precious savings in dollars, which she kept hidden in a closet. She and her sister had earned some of it selling homemade yogurt; the rest had come from Fico's father in Miami.

Nancy's parents suspected what was coming, but she didn't discuss her plans with them. There was a new seriousness about her, and she often retreated to her bedroom to listen to the radio. Although they spoke little, Nancy's mother understood that her daughter had to choose between her husband and the rest of her family. Intuitively, she knew what Nancy would do.

When Nancy left, she couldn't bear to say goodbye to her parents. Not a kiss, nothing. Her brother Luis had readied his bicycle. Nancy walked down the stairs of the apartment and lifted a leg over the rear of the bicycle, clinging to Luis.

From the balcony, Nancy's mother watched them go. Her daughter never looked back. Nancy told Luis she would send the family money once she arrived in the United States.

In the early morning darkness, she stepped from a riverbank into the makeshift boat at the port of Isabela de Sagua and joined thirty-one strangers, including six children and a pregnant woman. The group brought with them plenty of water and food, including an entire roasted pig, cheese, bread, and crackers.

The engine started up and the boat moved out into the sea. But the group soon learned that when drops of water fell into the vertical exhaust pipe, the motor stalled. When one of the spark plugs burned out, Nancy swam to shore with one of the young men to look for a wrench to change the spark plug. They found one and made the repairs, and with the engine running again, the group headed for a small cay off the coast where they stopped, ate lunch, and then resumed their journey.

Nancy knew that American ships were picking up boat people off the coast, and although her group's goal was to reach the shores of Florida, she hoped one of those ships would take her to the naval base at Guantánamo Bay so that she could find Fico. She felt relief that her journey was finally underway as the coastline disappeared in the distance.

The boat had two levels filled with passengers. Nancy sat on the upper level at the stern. At first people kept quiet, but in the rolling swells people soon began to vomit. Water was leaking in, and men started bailing with plastic water bottles that they had cut open at the tops. In the late afternoon, one man who was tending to the engine cried out in pain. A spinning shaft protruding from the motor had wounded him in the foot. Others tried to help him, but there was little they could do to treat his wound.

The boat had a deep hull and was unstable because it didn't have enough weight aboard. It leaned easily to either side if the passengers weren't evenly distributed, and there was one large man from Santa Clara who drew protests from others every time he shifted his weight.

"If you keep moving, it's going to flip over!" Nancy told everyone at one point. "Sit still or it's going to flip over."

Few on the boat were strong swimmers. Nancy began to wonder what she was doing there in the first place, and how she could have been so crazy. If only she had thought twice about getting on this boat! When night fell, the lights of ships appeared on the horizon, and people shouted out excitedly. The lights remained distant, and the men took turns bailing as the boat drifted across the dark water. They hoped to reach Cay Sal in the Bahamas, but there was no sign of the island.

Then someone saw it—a light finally drawing near. It was a fishing boat. The Cuban rafters drew up alongside the boat, and Nancy and the others leapt aboard, waking the crew of Bahamian lobster fishermen. The Cubans would be safe there until the Coast Guard came for them.

In the darkness, Nancy turned and watched their boat sinking. She had entrusted it with her life, and now she watched as it disappeared into the sea.

13

Guantánamo

All of the Cubans plucked from the sea by U.S. Coast Guard ships were being taken to Guantánamo Bay Naval Base, a hilly expanse at the mouth of the bay separated from Cuban territory by a no-man's-land of fences and land mines. The Americans planned to hold the Cubans there until they could decide how to deal with them.

Guantánamo Bay had been under U.S. control since 1898, when Marines seized the shoreline during the Spanish-American War. The U.S. government signed a lease agreement in 1903 and stayed after the triumph of Fidel Castro's revolution without asking permission. The lease agreement included a provision that the arrangement could be terminated only by mutual consent.

Castro once called the outpost "a dagger plunged into the heart of Cuban soil." When he ordered the base's water supply cut off in 1964, the U.S. military responded by building a desalination plant that eventually made the base self-sufficient. And so it remained—an odd relic of early-twentieth-century U.S. military history that had taken on a new role as a holding cell for people whose fate was yet to be determined.

Fico was among the first Cuban boat people to arrive in August 1994 at Guantánamo. The Cubans joined thousands of Haitians who had fled their country and were being held in separate camps spread across the base. The Cubans soon grew accustomed to sleeping on cots in military-style tents. They also adapted to the climate on the base, a dry and desolate landscape unlike any they had ever seen, with cactus rising from fields of golden-brown grass and iguanas sunning themselves on the pavement. By day their fenced encampment baked under a searing sun, but at night a cool breeze blew in from the deep waters offshore.

Before going to bed one night, Fico was brushing his teeth at an outdoor sink as he looked out over a field where sailors were clearing dry brush. His mind wandered home, to the people he left behind, to Nancy. He wondered where she was, and if she knew where he was.

The next morning he looked out across the same field as he brushed his teeth. It was completely covered with the green tents of a new camp. There must have been hundreds of them, all put up in one night. To accommodate the influx of Cubans, the military covered the base with tent cities. Tents eventually sprang up on the withered golf course, and covered an entire airstrip as well. Hundreds more people arrived each week.

Out at sea, the Coast Guard ship that had picked up Nancy and her group continued on for days, rescuing other boat people. The ship eventually transported them to an aircraft carrier where they joined crowds of refugees filling the huge decks. About 3,000 Cubans were loaded aboard the carrier heading for Guantánamo.

Nancy arrived more than a week after she left Isabela de Sagua. She stepped off the ship with the crowd of émigrés, most of them men. Each Cuban was issued a plastic bracelet that looked at first glance like a child's wristwatch. It had a smooth, black face and carried inside a number that could be read electronically. Nancy couldn't see her number, but she soon memorized it after hearing it read to her by the American troops.

In her camp, she slept in a tent with fifteen other people. She made friends, read newspapers in English when she could find them, and began to adjust to the new surroundings. But she felt uneasy inside the chain-link fences and was desperate to find Fico.

The camps were given names by letter—Camp Alpha, Camp Bravo, Camp Charlie, and so on. Nancy's new home was one of the last ones built, Camp Oscar. Like other camps, it was surrounded with fences topped with coils of razor wire. Hundreds were living inside, and when it rained, the earth turned to mud that oozed between Nancy's toes in her sandals.

At night, it was normal to see hutias—large, furry rodents that American sailors called "banana rats"—scurrying past the camp. Nancy heard that men in some other camps hunted the animals and ate them.

During the day, Nancy could see the Caribbean glimmering in the distance through the fence. Waves sounded against jutting rocks along the cliffs, though the shoreline was hidden from view below.

She went to the camp gate early each morning to try to talk to those who passed by, to ask about her husband and find out where he might be. She spent the morning there, then left for lunch and returned in the afternoon. At the end of each day, Nancy bathed with a bucket of water and went to bed not knowing anything more of Fico's whereabouts.

At the time Fico was living in a camp known as La India, where he had taken the job of camp *jefe* because he was motivated to help resolve the Cubans' daily problems and knew enough English to communicate with the Americans. The work kept him busy, which helped him cope. He had no idea where Nancy was, and communication between camps was difficult even if he had known where to find her.

He thought at first that perhaps she was still in Sagua la Grande. But as the flood of people poured into Guantánamo, he began to believe otherwise. Knowing Nancy, he thought she must have tried to leave. He worried about what could have happened during the journey.

Fico filled out a form used to locate relatives. The Americans made copies of the forms and posted them on bulletin boards. Men in his camp crowded around the bulletin boards to look for family members. Fico looked every day, but none of the forms posted were from Nancy. Fico hadn't seen her in nearly two months when a young man who worked for the Justice Department came and showed him a piece of paper.

"Federico, I think I have a surprise for you here," he said. "Look. You're the only Federico I know in Guantánamo. She must be yours."

He looked at the form. It was Nancy's handwriting.

"Yes, that's my wife," Fico said excitedly. "Where did you find her?"

"Let's go," the young man said. "I'll take you to see her."

When the two arrived at her camp in a jeep, they parked outside the gate in a cloud of dust. Hundreds of people inside crowded against the chain-link fence. As Fico got out of the jeep, he heard a voice call out: "Fiqui! Fiqui!" It was Nancy, leaning against the fence, gripping it. She was wearing flip-flops and was covered in grime and dust. She seemed to have lost thirty pounds, but Fico thought she looked wonderful. They touched hands through the fence.

"Are you okay?" Fico asked. "What are you doing standing here?"

"Just seeing if someone I knew passed by so I could send you a message or something," she replied.

The guards opened the gate and Fico hurried to her. As they embraced, he finally let go of the fear. The next day Fico returned to Nancy's camp with his belongings to move in.

Along with everyone else in the camps, they adapted to living with only the basic necessities. The Americans rationed the water, allowing people to bathe during fixed hours. U.S. troops ate at the local McDonald's and watched Hollywood movies at an outdoor theater, but the Cubans were generally confined to their camps. Some passed the time by doing volunteer work, helping to put up tents or taking turns cleaning the portable latrines.

There were others with no such civic responsibility, tattooed young men recently released from prison who bragged they were bound for "*la Yuma*"—slang for the United States. They robbed the sailors of their food, and had difficulty explaining to the Americans why they wanted to leave Cuba. Many of them were placed in a high-security zone called Camp X-Ray.

Fico thought the ex-convicts posed a major problem and something had to be done about them. In one interview with a television crew from Miami, he said the military authorities should do a thorough "purification" to determine those who should stay and those who should be sent back to Cuba. "When that selection is made, the U.S. government should return the ones with problems to the Cuban government and simply hold them where they need to be," Fico said.

Guantánamo served as a sieve, and the Americans eventually strained out hundreds of convicted criminals and sent them back to Cuba. About 1,200 were returned, including those who had committed crimes in Cuba and those who had broken the rules at Guantánamo.[1]

Others who remained in Nancy's camp organized a school for the children, began English classes for the adults, set up a barbershop, and played volleyball and basketball in their free time. She and Fico had been moved to a camp called McCalla that was set up on the tarmac of an airfield next to the bay. Across the water, they could see jets landing and taking off from a distant airstrip.

At the peak of the Guantánamo operation, 29,000 Cubans and 21,000 Haitians were living in tent cities strewn across the base.[2] Shipments of toys arrived from Miami for the children. Food in sealed packages was flown in from the United States. Nancy learned that the caramel-colored bags contained meals of chicken, tuna, and ham. Everyone wanted the ham, which was in short supply in Cuba at the time, so the people raffled off the ham meals by writing numbers on scraps of paper and drawing lots.

The rations also included cigarettes, which became a sort of currency in the camps. During elections for camp *jefe*, one candidate tried to buy votes with cigarettes. Others used cigarettes to bet at a game room that was set up in certain tents at night. The makeshift casino had roulette, bingo, and a lottery. Nancy joked that it was like a miniature Las Vegas.

Being held in the camps took a toll on the captives. Some who were particularly desperate drank gasoline or wounded themselves in hopes of getting out with a doctor's recommendation. Others went on hunger strikes in hopes of pressuring the military into letting them leave for the United States. Everyone wanted to see a doctor, and it was confusing as to who really needed one. In Nancy and Fico's camp, one woman had an asthma attack and died while she waited for treatment. A few people lost hope and tried to hang themselves.

But the way Nancy saw it, being in this halfway world was preferable to being in Cuba. She felt confident everything would work out. To pass the time, she asked a man who ran the mail service if she could help as a volunteer.

"If there's a chance for me to work with the mail, I'd like to work because I really get bored here in the *cabaña*," she told him.

Nancy carried the letters to the tents, arranged in rows of A, B, C and columns of 1, 2, 3.

When phones were installed, Fico and Nancy called their parents and told them not to worry, saying they were hopeful that they would eventually be able to leave. Their chance came when the Americans offered a medical "parole" to Fico's uncle, who had cancer and also happened to be in the camp. U.S. immigration authorities arranged for Fico and Nancy to leave with him and his wife.

After three months of captivity, Nancy and Fico boarded a plane for Miami. It was Nancy's first time flying. She was struck by the shortness of the trip, and yet in many ways Miami seemed so far away from all that she had known. She felt a bit frightened of the unknown as the plane touched down in Homestead, south of Miami. It was December 16, 1994. She and the others were handed immigration forms and were soon rolling across the tarmac in a school bus, their hair tousled by the air rushing in through the half-open windows.

The bus stopped next to a hangar near a crowd of waving people. One of them held up a small Cuban flag. Fico's father, who hadn't seen his son in years, was crying as the two stepped off the bus. Fico and Nancy were in shock. They hugged Fico's father, his wife, and two of Nancy's aunts. Then they rode off in a car to stay with their relatives, who cooked a special meal of *arroz con pollo* to welcome them at a party with friends.

Riding along on the wide highways, Nancy saw a consumerist world of towering billboards, glowing neon, and shiny office buildings. The sense of amazement lasted for months. Whenever Nancy went out, she often asked her relatives, "And that place, what is it? Does it belong to the government?" They explained that most everything she saw was privately owned.

As the Guantánamo crisis unfolded, Eloy Gutiérrez Menoyo urged President Clinton to take a different approach toward Castro. In a letter on August 31, 1994, he told the American president, "The time has come to negotiate."

"To think that the problems between the U.S. and Cuba are limited to the sphere of immigration is like trying to cover up the sun with one finger," he wrote.

Eloy mentioned that a delegation had visited the island on behalf of his group Cambio Cubano in April. Patricia went in his place, meeting alone with Castro and delivering a private letter on behalf of her father.

Eloy was making plans to travel to Cuba himself, and he soon learned his insistence could prove dangerous. The FBI warned him of a plot to rig his car with a bomb, so he and Gladys began to restrict their movements around town in Miami.

Eloy's friend Antonio Veciana, with whom he had formed Alpha 66, was among those who warned him against going out. But one day Eloy decided he wanted to stop by a restaurant on Calle Ocho in the heart of Cuban Miami, and it seemed there was no stopping him.

"I'm going to have a coffee. Who's coming with me?" he asked several friends before heading for his white Pontiac Grand Prix. When he arrived, some patrons at the restaurant booed him, but Eloy was unmoved.

"Calle Ocho doesn't interest me," he said. "I'm interested in Cuba."

Eloy had tried armed resistance, and now he was determined to try peace. Some in Miami said he was a quixotic dreamer if he thought talking to Castro would change anything.

Nancy and Fico moved in with Fico's father for their first few months in Miami. They were penniless. After a couple of weeks, and with the help of his family, Fico found a job as a quality-control worker at a company that sold airplane parts. Finding a job for Nancy took more time. She was anxious to get started.

"Even if it's picking tomatoes, I want to go work—anything," she told her father-in-law.

Nancy eventually found a job as a caseworker in a program helping newly arrived Cuban immigrants from Guantánamo. It was called the Guantánamo Refugee Assistance Project, or GRASP. She helped people in Guantánamo contact their families, and then went to the airport to meet them and help them in the transition. Most applied for political asylum.

Fico and Nancy entered the country on a "parole document" that later allowed them to request permanent resident status.

Nancy and Fico with their first car in Miami, 1995. (Courtesy of Nancy Lledes)

The U.S. government, meanwhile, signed immigration accords with Cuba ostensibly aimed at trying to prevent a future exodus. From now on, the U.S. authorities agreed to send back Cubans picked up at sea, unless they could prove a realistic fear of persecution. It was called the "wet-foot, dry-foot" policy. Those who set foot on U.S. soil would be allowed to request to stay in the United States, while those picked up at sea would generally be sent back. The new rules made it more difficult for Cubans to attempt the voyage to Florida by sea, but some kept trying.

After living with Fico's father for a time, Nancy and Fico moved into a one-bedroom apartment in the neighborhood of Little Havana. It was in a small building on Southwest Ninth Street within walking distance of coffee counters and cigar shops. Out front, Fico parked their gray 1986 Mazda, which he had bought from his stepmother for a thousand dollars. He used the car to get to work, while Nancy took the bus. Sometimes they woke in the morning to the sound of neighbors' children bouncing a basketball in the building. Their neighbors would knock on the door at any hour, sometimes just to chat. Asking all sorts of questions, they reminded Nancy of her neighbors back in Cárdenas who belonged to the Committee for the Defense of the Revolution. Apart from the new cars whooshing by, for Nancy it was almost as if their new home could have been in Cuba.

14

Facing Castro

Eloy had planted three palm trees in front of his house in Miami, one for each of his sons: five-year-old Carlos Alberto, two-year-old Alejandro José, and one-year-old Miguel Ángel. The boys meant everything to him. But at the same time, Eloy felt he had unfinished business back in Cuba.

As part of his efforts to arrange a meeting with Fidel Castro, Eloy sent Gladys to Havana as an emissary in March 1995. She traveled with the boys and met with Ricardo Alarcón, the National Assembly president. She also spoke to Castro by telephone, passing along her husband's request for a face-to-face meeting. Whenever Eloy made contact with the Cuban government, he tried to keep it confidential because speaking publicly about his belief in dialogue tended to bring swift consequences in Miami: he would be mocked on the radio shows, and his family would have to deal with threatening phone calls from anonymous enemies.

Eloy finally arranged to visit the island in June 1995 for a conference on "participatory democracy." Castro used the term to describe direct citizen participation in government decision-making, which he argued was a hallmark of the revolution and a key ingredient of socialism. He said Cuba's one-party system was more democratic than those of other countries because voter turnout was consistently near-perfect and elections didn't involve heavy campaign spending.[1] Elections held every five years selected the Communist Party's candidates to serve in the National Assembly, and they in turn affirmed Castro as president of the Council of State. Eloy saw nothing democratic in Castro's system, but the conference on democracy provided the opportunity he had been waiting for. He traveled to Havana with a group of about a dozen Cubans who shared his views.

Word of their trip spread quickly through Miami. Gladys heard a man making serious-sounding threats on the radio and decided to write to the FBI. "The caller expressed to the moderator . . . that 'a clandestine cell under the name X.16 has been created to punish people like Menoyo!' The caller expressed that they will use any means 'to punish' Menoyo," she wrote. "Needless to say, I am concerned for the well-being of my family." Days passed, however, and the threats didn't come to pass.

Eloy, meanwhile, was in Havana waiting for his chance to meet Fidel. "We bring a message that war belongs to the past," Eloy told one reporter who interviewed him in his hotel room.[2]

On the night of June 18, 1995, Eloy attended a reception at a government protocol house in Havana and joined invited guests on a terrace among columns festooned with vines.[3] Eloy wore a white dress shirt open at the collar and a blue blazer. He was sipping watermelon juice from a glass when Fidel strode onto the terrace in his olive fatigues, smiling. Faces turned as Fidel personally greeted each visitor.

"Eloy, how are you? I'm happy to see you here." They shook hands.

"I'm happy to be here," Eloy replied.[4]

Eloy was sixty and Fidel was sixty-eight. The two hadn't met face-to-face in thirty years.

Eloy retreated to a corner of the terrace as Fidel made his rounds in the crowd. Then Fidel reappeared.

"You've let your hair grow long," he told Eloy.

"It's not my style, but my wife likes it long, so long it is," Eloy admitted.[5]

Before parting for the night, they agreed they had much more to discuss.

The next day, they met privately for more than three hours in an office at the Conventions Palace, along with Foreign Minister Roberto Robaina and top aide Felipe Pérez Roque. As Eloy recalled that conversation, he pressed his points that all Cubans should have a right to visit their homeland and that opposition parties should be permitted. Although he had come as an adversary, Eloy no longer felt angry toward Fidel. He knew Fidel's tendency to monopolize conversation, so he asked to be allowed to do the talking. He had much to say. Fidel agreed.

"And let me tell you, I'm not a CIA agent," Eloy said, prompting laughter from Fidel.

Eloy said he wanted to move back to Havana with his wife and children,

Eloy meets Fidel in Havana, 1995. (AP/Wide World Photos)

to open an office on behalf of Cambio Cubano and start a legitimate political opposition. As Eloy recalled it, Fidel told him he would consider it.
Eloy also talked of political philosophy. He told Fidel he believed in a revolution "as Cuban as the palms," of peace, prosperity, and freedom—and
not of dictatorship. He suggested that Fidel, as leader of the revolution,
was in fact its first dissident in having strayed from its spirit.

"I still believe in that revolution," Fidel said.

"So why don't you take back the reins of the revolution? There is no
longer a communist bloc," Eloy retorted.

They finished their meeting without any solid commitments but with
an apparent openness on Fidel's part that Eloy sensed left the door open
for future talks. Only time would tell whether Fidel would entertain any
of Eloy's demands.

"The conversation was very frank and there were no limits of any
kind," Eloy told a reporter from *El Nuevo Herald*. "The world changes,
times change, and in this country changes are needed that cannot be
waited for with arms crossed."[6]

Threats against Eloy continued to arrive in letters and on postcards. He accumulated a stack of them in his office, holding the pile together with a rubber band. Eloy felt the attacks must have come from resentful Batista supporters who had lost everything they owned when they left Cuba decades ago. He was convinced that those threatening him were part of the same wealthy elite that once supported Batista's regime and its abuses. But Eloy was confident those hateful voices were fading with time.

When out on the streets in Miami, he sensed by facial expressions those who were his enemies. When Eloy spoke on the radio he often warned those who might try to harm him by saying, "Don't be mistaken: I am for a peaceful solution on the matter of Cuba, but I'm not a pacifist. If I meet someone in the street who believes he can come and use force, I know how to use it also, in spite of my age. I know how to defend myself."

Eloy kept a Smith & Wesson revolver in case he needed it, sometimes carrying the gun in his car's glove compartment.

Many Cuban exiles said they simply couldn't figure out what Eloy hoped to accomplish. They accused him of playing directly into Fidel's hands. Eloy had grown used to the critiques and was mentally prepared to fight them off. To those who said he was a Spaniard and not a Cuban, he said they were wrong. He was a Cuban patriot just as much as General Máximo Gómez, who had led Cuba's rebel army against the Spanish. Gómez, of course, was born Dominican.

Reflecting on the cause of trying to make peace, Eloy said, "What is beautiful, I believe, is to be capable—even after suffering—of burying the hatred."

Paquito found it invigorating to collaborate with talented musicians in New York. One such partnership began during a phone conversation with conductor and arranger Carlos Franzetti, an Argentine with a deep interest in Cuban music and jazz.

"You remember *Sketches of Spain*?" Franzetti asked, referring to the 1959 album by Miles Davis.

Paquito latched on to the idea right away. *Sketches of Spain* wasn't Spanish music but a jazz interpretation. In the same way, they agreed to collaborate on what Paquito would describe as "a jazz tribute to Cuban music, using elements of Cuban music." They called the album *Portraits of Cuba*. They met to record with a big band on a freezing day in February 1996 at St. Peter's Church in New York City. The music ranged from the

Paquito performing in New York, 2005. (Courtesy of Peter Svensson)

traditional "*Tú*"—a sweeping, triumphant *habanera* that was the first song Paquito ever played live—to his own compositions, such as the melancholy-tinged "Portraits of Cuba."

Chesky Records designed the CD cover to pay homage to Paquito's past, including black-and-white photographs of him performing as a boy. The album landed Paquito in the 1997 Grammy awards, where he waited in the audience while a woman opened an envelope to announce the prize for Best Latin Jazz performance: "And the Grammy goes to . . . Paquito D'Rivera, 'Portraits of Cuba'!"

With applause filling the hall, Paquito strode up to the stage wearing a black suit. He held the golden phonograph in his hands and took the microphone with a quick attempt at humor.

"Well, I have to speak in English now, and that's the hardest thing to do for me. I have only a hundred words in English, and fifty of them are dirty, so . . ." He lowered his head mischievously and peered over his wire-rimmed glasses.

"I remember that a couple of years ago I had to present an award to the great Cachao. And I say that it's hard to give an award to a man who is an award himself. And I had my award last year when Chesky gave me the opportunity to work with one of the greatest composers and arrangers that made possible this prize, the great Carlos Franzetti. You made this possible."

"Stand up! Carlos Franzetti," Paquito motioned into the crowd with a hand outstretched, then to everyone said with a smile, "*Gracias.* Thank you very much."

After arriving in Florida, Fico and Nancy began to work and save. They had brought no money or belongings with them from Cuba, and their salaries were low, but they saved as much as they could and made plans. Nancy felt that was the wonderful thing about this new country: there were no limits. When they had saved enough, Fico bought a used Ford Bronco and Nancy started driving the old Mazda instead of taking the bus.

They made room in their one-bedroom apartment for friends who arrived from Guantánamo to stay there temporarily. At one point, they were sharing the apartment with two of Fico's friends, David and Ricardo, plus Ricardo's brother. The visitors slept on the floor until they could move on to their own jobs and apartments.

Meanwhile, Nancy and Fico were saving up to buy their own house. In late 1997, they found a place within their price range in a rural area of southern Miami-Dade County. Fico's father had seen the house and recommended the area of avocado and mango orchards as peaceful. The house was on one acre planted with rows of avocado trees and fringed with coconut palms, orange, lychee, mango, banana, and loquat trees. The house had been built about 1930, and its original wooden walls were still standing despite the destruction of Hurricane Andrew in 1992, which had forced the previous owners to repair the badly damaged roof and carport.

The elderly couple had raised their children there, and the old man told of how, decades before, the cries of Florida panther cubs used to be heard in the forest. The idea of moving to an area with few neighbors and little commotion was appealing. Nancy and Fico soon made a down payment on the house. They pulled up the old carpets and began to make the place theirs.

Nancy felt pleased with their new home, but her thoughts often wandered back to Cuba and her family. She had nightmares of being suddenly trapped on the island. She floated back to her parents' house, to the immigration office, where she was told she didn't have permission to leave Cuba to come home. "But I don't fit here anymore. This isn't my place," she protested. For Nancy, those were the worst nightmares.

The office of Cambio Cubano was located on the second floor of a strip mall on Miami's Southwest Eighth Street. Visitors walked through a meeting area to get to Eloy's office, where portraits of Bill Clinton and Nelson Mandela hung on the walls. Curls of smoke rose from an ashtray while Eloy took calls at his desk and discussed strategy with close friends and followers.

At home, he and Gladys spent weekend afternoons by the pool with Carlos, Alex, and Miguel Ángel. The boys were going to public school, where they mostly spoke English. But at home Eloy usually spoke to them in Spanish. He and Gladys established Wednesday as their "English only" day. If Eloy slipped up and spoke Spanish, he lost a penny. If the boys strayed from Spanish on other days, they faced the dreaded possibility of losing video game time.

For Eloy, light moments with his sons offered respite from the pressures of his cause. He had met briefly with Fidel two other times after their encounter in June 1995, but Eloy's aim of creating a space for dissent in Cuba appeared as elusive as ever.

Sometimes he awoke at 3 a.m. when the house was quiet, slipped out of bed, and turned on the television in the living room. Flipping through the channels in the blue glow, Eloy's thoughts drifted as he analyzed the situation in Cuba without interruptions—its problems, the flaws of U.S. policies, what lay ahead. Just as he had done during the long years in prison, he transported himself away in thought.

15

Exile

When I met Nancy, Eloy, and Paquito in the late 1990s, they were living in Miami and New York, largely cut off from the island that remained their home at heart. As I began talking with them about their lives, I learned of the deep divisions they confronted and the inner conflicts that came as a result of their separation from Cuba. This was reflected in the fact that Eloy faced mountainous obstacles in trying to move back to the island, in the bitter jokes that Paquito told about life under "*El Comandante*," and in the way Nancy's eyes would well up with tears at the mention of her parents.

At that time, some people were optimistic that reconciliation was on the horizon. When Pope John Paul II visited Cuba in 1998, he prayed "that this land may offer to everyone a climate of freedom, mutual trust, social justice and lasting peace. . . . May Cuba, with all its magnificent potential, open itself up to the world, and may the world open itself up to Cuba."

The pope said Cubans on the island and in exile should work toward peace. He urged them to "follow a path of reconciliation, dialogue and fraternal acceptance." To the applause of hundreds of thousands in the Plaza de la Revolución, he declared: "This is the time to start out on the new paths."

But for Cubans divided for so many years, this was the most difficult of aims. A highly politicized rift appeared in Miami during the custody battle over the six-year-old boy Elián González, rescued at sea in an ill-fated crossing that claimed his mother's life. A political tug-of-war stretched nearly five months and ended on April 22, 2000, when federal agents stormed the home of Elián's Miami relatives. The raid was a first step toward returning the boy to his father on the island, which represented a painful defeat for staunch Castro opponents like Paquito, who saw this as a shameful surrender by the U.S. government. Hundreds of enraged protesters filled the streets of Little Havana, shouting at police, throwing rocks, and coughing through clouds of tear gas.

Another less vocal segment of Cuban exiles said it was only natural for the boy to be returned to his father. Eloy, in fact, had met Elián's father Juan Miguel in Washington and felt sorry for him. "The father is the father," Eloy put it simply. But if the threatening letters that Eloy once received were a barometer of public sentiment about his views, things appeared to be changing. Those letters had slowed to a trickle within a few years, and then they stopped coming altogether.

Five years after Nancy left Cuba, her mother obtained government permission to fly to Florida for a visit. That trip in the summer of 1999 was the first time her mother had ever left the island, and she was not tempted to emigrate. Aside from seeing her daughter and other relatives, she wasn't particularly interested in anything about the place. When they took a drive to Key West one weekend, she marveled at the high prices the American tourists were willing to pay for just about everything.

Nancy and her mother spent time together picking avocados behind the house. When Nancy had to go off to work, her mother sat out front selling the avocados on the roadside for a dollar apiece. Her mother was often surrounded by relatives, and she remarked that her month-long trip seemed almost like going away to see family in Havana. Her political views generally clashed with those of her relatives in Miami, so no one brought up politics.

"My only interest is to see my family, to see them and be with them here finally," Nancy's mother explained. "They have their life and I have mine. I'm happy in Cuba. Each of us has her own life, and each of us respects that."

When her mother returned home to Cuba, Nancy realized that neither she nor her mother had any idea when they might see each other again. It was a painful truth, but Nancy had little time to dwell on it. Her work kept her extremely busy. She started her days at 5 a.m. and listened to the radio while commuting to work, often flipping through stations broadcasting news, salsa, or talk shows before settling on soft rock in English.

She could spend nearly an hour in traffic on the way to the university where she worked at a human rights institute, helping newly arrived Cubans and other immigrants apply for asylum. Her days were hectic and her desk stacked with files.

"In Cuba," she explained with a smile, "there is time enough for everything. Time is long. Here time slips away like nothing. You run out fast."

Fico and Nancy were rarely alone in their house. Her sister came to live with them for a while, then it was a distant relative of Fico who arrived in Florida via speedboat, then Fico's brother, who arrived on a boat with his wife and two kids. Others followed, staying with Nancy and Fico while looking for jobs and places to live. In that way, Nancy and Fico were usually surrounded by Cubans making the same familiar transitions.

Often concerned about her family back in Cuba, Nancy sent her mother cash whenever acquaintances were traveling to the island. The U.S. trade embargo set yearly limits for remittances, but Nancy never sent enough to break the law. She wasn't particularly concerned about that anyway. She and her parents shared the view that the embargo made no sense.

"The people are the ones who are affected in reality," Nancy said. "It's also a justification for the Cuban government to say the situation is bad in Cuba due to the embargo."

Meanwhile, Castro declared that Cubans who supported his government were leading a "Battle of Ideas" and urged people to tighten their belts for the transition to a new, self-reliant economy.

On the road that cuts through the countryside to Sagua la Grande, the phrase "*Socialismo o muerte*" figured prominently among the slogans on walls and billboards I passed as I approached the town during a visit in 2001. There were few cars on the streets of Sagua la Grande. Most people took bicycles or walked. An occasional horse-drawn carriage served as a bus. In the second-story apartment where Nancy's parents lived, her mother sorted beans at the kitchen table while she explained why she believes in the revolution and Fidel Castro.

"I don't have much life left, but I hope I'm gone before Fidel. Because it would be so painful," she said. "He's a fighter, a fighter for the good of humanity."

During the 1950s she had read Fidel's *History Will Absolve Me* and believed her town needed to escape from poverty and police oppression.

Horse-drawn cart used for transport in Cienfuegos, 2005. (Ian James)

She took an active role as a rebel supporter, once spiriting a shotgun to young fighters who briefly took control of the city on April 9, 1958. She hid the shotgun under her arm and inside the sleeve of her blouse, carrying it out of her house to the rebels' hideout in a nearby building. She returned home safely, but most of the young men in the rebellion were hunted down and killed. She never forgot their sacrifice.

All these decades later, with her dark brown hair tinged with gray, she faced a different sort of struggle. Sometimes just finding eggs to eat could involve a long search from one market to another. But Nancy's mother said she accepted the inconveniences as sacrifices toward a higher purpose, and also believed the struggles made Cubans stronger. Economic troubles, she said, have "showed us how to work to get out of a problem, how to live with little and how to fight."

While she fried *tostones* for dinner, the television blared from the living room, where Benjamín habitually watched the state-run news from his rocking chair. At that time, the news was about Fidel celebrating his seventy-fifth birthday with President Hugo Chávez in Venezuela and criticism of a trial in Florida against five Cuban spies.

Nancy's mother said she believed in the "Battle of Ideas" proclaimed by Fidel. The battle can be won, she said, by countering the U.S. government's lies. She believed the five Cubans accused of spying were heroes. After all, she said, they were trying to find out about the plans of Cuban exiles "to attack us."

Some Cubans I had met elsewhere during my trip complained bitterly about poverty and the unchanging political system. But others such as Nancy's parents said they were happy and proud to be living in a country that provided for all people and was free of U.S. imperialism.

Nancy's mother introduced me to one elderly woman, a prominent Communist Party member, who proudly displayed photos of Fidel on the walls of her apartment. She showed off the machetes she used in the annual sugar harvest, saying she was grateful for the revolution because it had lifted her out of poverty, taught her to read, and made clear that women could be more than "prostitutes and maids." She said she had grown up in a dirt-floored shack and received her first pair of shoes at age fourteen.

"Today I live happily. I have everything," the woman said, smiling in an armchair in her modest apartment. "No one forces anyone here to be communists—no one."

Nancy's mother lamented that the younger generation didn't seem to appreciate the battles Fidel had fought on their behalf.

"The problem now is that we are all equal here. We receive the same opportunities for everything. All the children have the chance to study."

"Forty years have passed. Now the young don't know anything," she fretted. "At the moment what they see is discomfort, the necessities. And so they leave. They go away. They don't come to understand why we are like this. It must be explained."

Of her three children, only her son Luis remained in Cuba, working at the sugar mill in Sagua La Grande; her daughters were both in the United States.

"Sometimes I get sentimental when I'm alone," she said mournfully. "They chose that life. They chose."

Gazing into the distance, Nancy's mother added, "So much hope I had for my children, and I've ended up practically without them."

Nancy's mother on her second-story balcony in Sagua la Grande, 2005. (Ian James)

She said she no longer wrote many letters to Nancy. She had heard sometimes they went unopened for weeks, and she assumed it was because reading them could make her daughter feel sad.

Nancy, for her part, missed her parents dearly. In her backyard, she sat on a lawn chair talking about how her life had changed and reflecting on the system she had left behind in Cuba.

"It has parts that are good and parts, like anything, that are bad. The only bad thing I see in the system is that it limits you as a human being. It destroys your hopes."

In Florida she had been able to rebuild those hopes, despite the frustrations of paying bills and weathering long work days. She said she would love to go back to Cuba to visit someday, but never to live.

Paquito had a great deal of respect for Eloy Gutiérrez Menoyo, whom he had once met in Spain. But he also was mystified by Eloy's optimism that talking to Fidel Castro could make a difference.

"There is nothing else to talk about," Paquito said. "He's a dictator. He's *bla, bla.*"

For a time, Paquito's outspokenness made listening to his music in Cuba a subversive act. At the Punta del Este jazz festival in Uruguay in 2000, he spotted President Carlos Menem of Argentina in the audience and greeted him. "It's a pleasure to have a head of state here. Welcome, sir." Some in the audience applauded, while others booed, and Paquito blurted out, "That, in my country, cannot be done!"

Nostalgia was a constant part of life in exile for Paquito. Memories of Cuba returned in a flash one summer day in New Jersey, as Paquito stood in his kitchen talking on the phone with a friend. Pausing for a moment, he turned toward the window, gazing out toward trees in the yard. A storm was passing overhead, and heavy rain pattered on the roof—just like the thundering torrents he had seen in Cuba when dark clouds swept in from the sea.

"Wow! What a beautiful downpour!" Paquito exclaimed, stepping closer to the window while keeping the phone to his ear. "Brenda," he called out, "I've never seen a downpour like this here!"

The sound of torrential rain washed over the house. "*¡Coño! How*

beautiful this downpour is, a real good one! It makes me feel like I'm back in my country right now."

He stood looking out the window for a moment, marveling. *"¡Que lindo aguacero, carajo!* The trees should be very happy."

On one of his visits to Cuba, Eloy sneaked into La Cabaña with Gladys. Workers had been removing old prison bars from windows as they restored the fortress to turn it into a museum. The empty alleys, corridors, and galleries were eerily quiet, but Eloy's sons played happily in the fort, not knowing of their father's painful history there. A "Do Not Enter" sign blocked one path; Eloy went right past it. Gladys took snapshots with a point-and-shoot camera while he led her through, pointing out Galera 23A, where he had once been imprisoned.

"Just keep talking in English," he told her. "If anyone comes over and asks you anything, just ramble on in English."

Eloy urged her to change the film quickly once she finished one roll because the authorities could always confiscate the camera but were less likely to demand other rolls of film. No one stopped them.

Eloy explained what each room was used for, including cells where men were held in solitary confinement. He stopped at the mess hall, where the prisoners went for breakfast, and the rooftop, where they were led out for fresh air. They paused at the *paredón*, where men once fell before firing squads. Weeds grew between the crumbling, pitted stones in the fortress's walls.

Just as time was wearing away at the stone, it was taking a toll on Eloy. At sixty-five, he underwent surgery to repair a detached retina in his right eye—the one the guards had spared when they beat him years ago. Even after months of recovery, he could see only light and fuzzy shapes. He had a second operation, then a third in an attempt to save the eye. The surgeries failed.

A year later, he still couldn't read a newspaper without a special magnifying glass that made him dizzy. He could just make out the headlines by holding the paper very close to his face. By that time, his long-dormant left eye had begun to transmit a tiny bit of vision. Eloy figured his brain must have sent signals to that eye desperately seeking sight. He could no longer drive but could still stride confidently to greet a visitor with a handshake.

"Television, I can hear it but not watch it. The image is all blurry, as if I were driving a car across a bridge in London through a fog, a thick fog," he explained. "I'm not getting better. What I'm doing is adapting."

He continued his work, making speeches, sending out news releases, traveling to Washington to meet sympathetic members of Congress. Gladys took a part-time job at a discount store to help make ends meet. The boys played in the yard with their dog, a boxer named Gandhi, and Eloy began dictating his memoirs into a tape recorder.

Eloy exuded confidence in his cause, but he also appeared to be growing impatient with the lack of a response from the Cuban government. With Fidel's participation, Eloy felt a peaceful transition to democracy would be possible. But if Fidel were to die first, Eloy worried it could unleash a war for power and control. Eloy often repeated that his goal was to make sure the opposition had a place in society, but his requests to be allowed an office on the island remained unanswered.

Other dissidents, meanwhile, submitted a petition to parliament with thousands of signatures asking for a referendum on whether Cubans

Eloy with his boys in Miami, 2002. (Ian James)

should have guarantees to rights such as free speech and private business ownership. Castro's supporters countered the effort with their own petition drive, collecting millions of signatures for a proposal promptly approved by parliament that enshrined the island's socialist system as "irrevocable" and declared to the world that "capitalism will never return again to Cuba."[1] Many volunteers involved in the petition drive were

Carrying water in Trinidad, 2005. (Ian James)

among seventy-five dissidents who were arrested in 2003 and sentenced to long prison terms, accused of working with American officials to try to undermine the Cuban government. Those who went to prison denied the accusations.[2]

Across the Florida Straits, Eloy was lobbying the U.S. government to drop the embargo, which had already been loosened, allowing for sales of American food from rice to apples. He said it only served as an excuse for Castro. He also criticized what he saw as growing anarchy in Cuba. "The poor steal, everyone steals. They don't have any other option left."

Cubans call it *resolviendo*—struggling, stealing, finding a way to get what one needs. Though Cuba's doctors are highly trained, they often lack adequate supplies. Nancy knew this, and when her father needed to have his third hernia surgery, she sent him a sterile synthetic mesh from Miami to help keep the internal wound from breaking open again. Benjamín gave it to the surgeon, who inserted it before stitching shut the wound.

For some in Cuba, *resolviendo* has become a way of life. Workers steal screws and nails from their jobs to make their house repairs. Many buy beef from illegal suppliers who risk jail terms by slaughtering state cows for profit. Some Cubans blame the U.S. embargo. Others say it's due to the failings of Castro and the mish-mash of socialism and capitalism he has created.

"This system, in theory, is the best there is," Nancy's brother Luis told me during an outing to the family cabin at Uvero. "The problem is that human nature corrupts it. People want to be paid in money, food—not *conciencia*."

Standing in the breeze on a rickety pier where he and Nancy once watched dolphins jump in the distance, Luis recalled his sister's departure as a sad but inevitable event. She had given him a brave kiss on the cheek and then was gone. "She was my second mother," he recalled wistfully.

Luis hadn't seen her since that day in 1994 when she hopped on the back of his bicycle and they rode out of town on her way to the boat.

16

Return

Eloy was taking his family on a vacation to Cuba. It was the summer of 2003, and school was out. Gladys did the packing, filling suitcases with their clothes, sheets, towels, and toiletries. Eloy had made a special request to bring extra clothes this time.

"Gladys, when you go out to buy things for Cuba, I need you to buy me some clothes for a friend."

"What type?" she asked.

He thought about it, then said they would need two pairs of dress pants, one pair of jeans, shirts to go with them, underwear, socks, one pair of pajamas, a pair of tennis shoes, and a pair of dress shoes.

"And what sizes?"

"Just buy it all as if it were for me."

"Are you sure?"

"Yes, if it doesn't fit, there is always someone else to give it to."

They planned a trip much like previous ones and booked a room at the Hotel Neptuno, where they always stayed. Eloy used the time to talk to most everyone he met about the situation on the island and the sorts of changes they felt were needed. The vacation went according to plan—sightseeing in the lush valley of Viñales, swimming in a waterfall pool, taking the boys to the beach. It ended much like other previous trips. At the airport, a group of reporters gathered to hear what Eloy had to say as he left.

It was early morning and their son Carlos felt queasy, so Gladys stayed a few steps back with him outside the airport while Eloy stood talking with the journalists. As Carlos sat slumped on the curb and Gladys was asking him if he needed to go to the bathroom, Alex hurried over and asked, "Mom, what is that Dad is saying? He wants to stay here and work?!"

Eloy explained his decision to reporters succinctly and handed them a written statement with everything he had to say. He hadn't told a soul until now. Gladys broke into tears. Eloy turned around, gave her a kiss, and said, "Get into the airport with the kids. I'm going to stay."

Gladys checked in for the flight, telling the airline employee they were five passengers. In her shock, it hadn't registered that only four would be leaving. Later she realized the clothes Eloy had asked her to bring weren't for a friend at all; they were for him. Even months later, her mind was filled with questions about why he hadn't told her.

"I support what he's doing, but if he would have asked me I would have told him, 'No, don't do it that way,'" she said. "So maybe he was trying to avoid that. Maybe he was trying to make his going away a little bit easier."

In the papers he handed to reporters, Eloy explained his decision. He had kept it a secret to make sure nothing got in the way. Although he would not be living with his family, he said,

> I harbor the hope that they can be reunited with me here in the not-too-distant future. In the same way, I also hope that one day Cubans can freely enter and leave their country without needing a visa.
>
> My decision not to return to exile and to settle in Cuba for good is the direct result of a deep and deliberate analysis of the country's situation and an understanding that I could be more useful here than abroad. From a legal standpoint, I am not breaking the law. As a peaceful activist, my action shouldn't be seen as a challenge. I come to work . . . for the peace and reconciliation of all Cubans.

He said Cuba had been in one long struggle since its fight for independence.

> On January 1, 1959, our island astonished the planet with the triumph of a revolution that seemed to have defeated all the forces of evil. . . . We trusted that there wouldn't be another historic turn of fate that could hold back our progress or hold hostage our peace. It hasn't turned out that way.
>
> We have been fragmented as a country, as a people, as a nation, as a family. . . . The glorious splendor of the revolution of January 1, 1959 was

summed up in a motto that was a collective wish: "Freedom with bread, and bread without fear." For many reasons, the bread never arrived and the absence of certain fundamental freedoms has been too painful to justify a complex government platform that has reached a disproportionate level of disfavor before the patient bitterness of the island's people.

On June 19, 1995, I met with President Fidel Castro, a hopeful meeting that in its moment took on importance, not only for having a special historic meaning but also because both of us were showing signs of overcoming political enmity and apparently insurmountable personal differences. My record as a revolutionary commander who turned into an opponent and who spent 22 years of crude political imprisonment—modestly put—gave the meeting with the head of the Cuban government, and all it stood for, an implicit importance, precisely due to the implausibility of the meeting. We were, to a certain point, a metaphor of what the nation could and should do for its reconciliation.

"I came out of my meeting with Fidel hopeful," Eloy said. But his outlook dimmed over time. "Things didn't turn out the way they should have. Years passed, and our meetings with officials of the Cuban government didn't produce the legal space that Cambio Cubano had made its demand and banner. . . . Today, good faith brings me here with the aim of recovering lost time."

He spoke of the obstacles he felt had impeded the way, including the U.S. government's policies of "sponsoring an opposition that becomes weaker and weaker as it is perceived to be more closely linked to Washington."

Nevertheless, it's time for Cubans who love the nation to take a step forward that will allow us to find revolutionary ways of getting out of this situation. That's what I propose to do starting this instant.

Cuba is, in spite of everything, a beautiful and cheerful land, a garden generous with its colors, a marvelous paradise that captivates its own people and others. It's worth fighting for!

I am returning home. I don't remember, nor do I wish to remember, how long I have been away. There was a time when to say Cuba for me was to say forever. It was to name the place where I would remain happy until death. This is also the feeling of thousands of exiles. To return today is to appeal for the wish that there may be no more exiles or breaks between Cubans. May our family be one.

I return to work here for a legal space where we can build a future of plurality and coexistence. It is also time to stop putting off the prosperity that Cubans deserve.

The job that awaits us is extremely complex. I think about Gandhi, I think about Martin Luther King. I think about Mandela and César Chavez. I think, in relative terms, of José Martí and his clear and simple message for Cuba: "With all and for the good of all."

Nothing will lead me away from the path of peace. I am pleased to know that I am not alone in this effort. I know that, as on January 1, 1959, this nation will bring about the miracle of reconciliation.

I believe the journey in search of a new revolution begins today.

Nearly two years after his historic return, I met Eloy at his father's old apartment in Havana. We sat talking in the living room, sipping strong coffee while he smoked Hollywood cigarettes, pulling one after another out of the red box. Eloy was staying in the apartment at the invitation of a family friend who had been living there for decades.

He said he regularly held meetings with a consular official assigned to his case at the foreign ministry, insisting he should be given legal status in the country, assigned a home, permitted access to the news media and the Internet, and granted permission to start an independent opposition party.

"Up until now I haven't been told 'no' to anything, but also I haven't been told 'yes' to anything. So I'm basically in limbo," he explained. Eloy faced difficulties with both the Cubans and the Americans. The U.S. Interests Section had sent him a letter warning that as a U.S. resident he could be fined up to $250,000 and sentenced to ten years in prison for staying in Cuba and violating the embargo.

"What's absurd from my point of view is that I'm not here as a tourist, I'm here demanding freedoms in this country," Eloy said.

The embargo prevented his family from visiting at that time, and Eloy didn't want his sons to live in Cuba under the circumstances anyway. During phone calls, the boys—at that time eleven, thirteen, and sixteen—brought Eloy up to date on their latest activities, from playing steel drums to meeting girls. They asked their father questions to which there were no easy answers: "So, *Pipo*, when are you coming home? When will we see you?"

As usual, Eloy faced great uncertainties and was sandwiched between opposing political camps. He could be just as critical of Washington as he was of Castro. He called it blatantly wrong that the Americans were using Guantánamo Bay to imprison their enemies from around the world indefinitely, and argued that U.S. aid to Cuban dissidents played directly into Castro's hands by making them appear to be mercenaries. The way Eloy put it, "I'm between the extreme right of the exile community, the U.S. government, and the extreme left of this country."

Nevertheless, he said he was meeting plenty of Cubans who shared his views and was regularly signing up handfuls of new members to join Cambio Cubano. Delegations of American congressmen and European parliamentarians sought out Eloy for meetings. Journalists and writers did so too, including his friend Gabriel García Márquez.

The government appeared to ignore Eloy for the most part, but he was certain he was being closely monitored and his phones were tapped.

"We're living under a dictatorship here," he said. "Everything is controlled."

He said the worst aspects of the system could be seen in the "salaries of hunger" paid to Cubans. Eloy thought it was shameful that some had to survive on as little as eight dollars a month. He also could not understand why Cubans weren't permitted at many hotels and beaches reserved for foreign tourists. He was furious when one hotel refused to serve him lunch because he couldn't produce a foreign passport.

"It's total rubbish," Eloy said. "With a passport or without, you have the same right to eat in a restaurant."

He noted that the new generation was growing up in a country where those with access to dollars or euros could live a class above the rest.

As we stepped out onto the street from the apartment, Eloy spotted a young woman wearing jean shorts and bright white sneakers. He quietly remarked, "Look, she has family outside the country." The rest of Eloy's thought was unstated but clear: otherwise, she wouldn't be able to afford such luxuries. As for himself, Eloy received modest sums from his daughter in Puerto Rico to help cover expenses. He found it hard to understand how others made do.

"The country is stuck," he said. "The country can never progress like this. The salaries aren't enough to afford anything, so people have to be stealing."

Eloy learned that thieves had even penetrated the National Archives. One street vendor had offered to sell him an old photograph of himself, but Eloy promptly turned down the offer when he noticed "National Archives of Cuba" stamped on the back. A card catalog at the National Archives still held a card listing photos of Eloy, describing him simply as a "traitor to the fatherland."

Eloy felt that others bore the blame for betraying the country's hopes. "What exists here, you can classify it as a society of slavery, just that, but one can't talk about socialism or revolution. Revolution represents change."

For Eloy, Havana's crumbling buildings, potholed streets, and broken water pipes were symbols of how little change there had been. He took a stroll around the uneven dirt track at the waterfront Parque de Martí, gazed upward at the paint peeling from the stands, and remarked, "This used to be beautiful."

There were few cars on the country road leading to Sagua la Grande during my visit in the summer of 2005—just an occasional Moskvich or Lada, and now and then a farm tractor pulling a trailer filled with passengers. A sign on the road leading into town announced "Revolution—is to change everything that should be changed—is to defend values."

A reggaeton beat blared from doorways in town, while people crouched to fill buckets of water at maintenance holes along the sidewalk where they could reach the pipes. Young men with earrings sat on a curb, sharing a bottle of rum.

Little appeared to have changed at the second-story apartment of Nancy's parents. They welcomed me warmly with hugs, and I sat talking with Nancy's mother at the kitchen table next to her humming 1951 Frigidaire while Benjamín watched television in the living room.

"Tomorrow it should be our turn for the blackout because we didn't have one today," she said. Often the power would go out for six hours at night or six hours in the morning, but she said she was hopeful the situation would improve once the government finished upgrading its power plants in the coming months.

She showed me to the guest room. Benjamín explained I should be careful to turn off the water completely after washing; if not, trickling

Benjamín watching a speech by Fidel Castro on television in his home in Sagua la Grande, 2005. (Ian James)

water would empty the rooftop tank, and they would have to start up the motor to pump more water up from the street.

Nancy's mother showed me photos she had brought back from a recent month-long trip to Miami—snapshots at the beach, at the aquarium, and with flamingos. She said Nancy had wanted her to stay for three months, but it wasn't possible because Benjamín, now seventy-five, had health problems and needed help at home. He had recovered from multiple hernia operations, but to soothe other aches and pains he prepared a gel from aloe vera that grew on the terrace. His hands trembled as he skinned the aloe with a dull knife.

Nancy's mother said she had received 600 dollars from her daughter before returning home and had put the money in the bank. She withdrew about forty dollars each month to help buy food and pay other expenses. At the same time, the government had raised pension payments, bringing her and Benjamín a steady income of 490 pesos a month.

"We aren't bad off," she said. "Many people have less."

Nancy's mother heard plenty of denigrating comments about the Cuban government while in Florida, but she didn't let it get to her. She was stopped for two hours at the Miami airport by an immigration agent who insisted on gauging her views, saying Fidel Castro had become one of the world's richest men after so many years in power, and what did she think about that?

One Cuban man she met in Miami demanded to know why Benjamín hadn't come along too. "They all talk trash," Nancy's mother said. She let it go in one ear and out the other. The purpose of her trip had been simply to see her family, and nothing else mattered.

In the afternoon sunshine, she hung white rags on her clothesline after washing them. "It's for a friend of mine who doesn't have water, so I help her out," she explained. Nancy's mother also did volunteer work at the municipal committee of the Communist Party, and lately she had received plenty of complaints from people upset about the blackouts, demanding to know when they could expect the situation to improve.

"Everybody sees the party as if it were God, as if it could resolve all the problems," she said. She assured people repairs to the power plants were underway, and once they were finished, the blackouts would lessen. "Last

Nancy's mother doing laundry at her home in Sagua la Grande, 2005. (Ian James)

year there was a serious problem. The blackouts weren't planned like they are now," she said while sewing a blouse at the kitchen table.

The next day, the lights went out promptly at 6 p.m., and Nancy's mother lit a kerosene lamp while Benjamín sat in the dark in the living room, listening to 1950s ballads on a battery-powered radio. They said they used to have a converter to keep the lights on, but it was broken. Only street lamps remained lit, and people pulled chairs out onto their balconies and sidewalks to talk until it was time to go to sleep.

During one of our conversations, Nancy's mother said she was proud of how her country had stood up to U.S. aggression for so many years and had survived despite the American embargo and the fall of the Soviet Union.

"Tough times passed, but we lifted ourselves up bit by bit," she said. "I really have a lot of faith that all of this will get better, better and better."

She said it may take time, but the revolution will prevail. And when Fidel dies, others will carry on the system he has created, she predicted. "There is a beautiful future here."

The phone rang while we sat talking, and Nancy's mother answered: "*Oigo.* . . ."

It was Nancy calling with good news: she hoped to travel to Cuba soon, once she had received her entry visa.

"How great, how great," her mother said delightedly. She had known Nancy was trying to come, but she hadn't known when it would be possible.

"We'll see," Nancy's mother said after hanging up. If it worked out, she said, it would be her daugther's first trip home in eleven years. Gazing out the window, she reflected on the possibility.

"The phone calls make me happy. Those are the things that fill me up."

Nancy and Fico had waited ten years after they arrived in Florida to apply for U.S. citizenship. Because they were once members of the Communist Youth, the law required them to wait a decade before they could be eligible. While her application was pending, Nancy sent off paperwork to apply for a Cuban passport, which she would need to travel back to visit her parents. Fico had no interest in returning to Cuba as the situation stood, but Nancy felt the time had come to see her family after so many years apart, so she planned to make the trip alone.

When she finally left for her two-week visit in April 2006, she did not see it as a leisure trip but rather as a chance to reconnect with her parents and help them with several pressing issues. She planned to help fix up their apartment, which had a leaking roof and walls that badly needed a paint job. She also brought money she had saved for them and hoped to deal with paperwork to help her father arrange a future visit to see her in Florida. Nancy wanted to do everything she could to make that possible.

She had prepared herself mentally to see her hometown with different eyes—its rundown buildings and the daily struggles its people faced. But she felt sorry that her parents put what money they had into basic sustenance while her brother Luis had to work a second job raising pigs to provide for his family. She sensed that many of her old friends clearly wanted something more in their lives but saw little opportunity and nowhere to go.

One afternoon, Nancy invited three old friends from high school to a lunch of ham sandwiches and beer at a fast-food restaurant called *El Rápido*. She knew they could not afford to eat there on their own meager salaries in Cuban pesos, and when they had finished, her friend Blanca asked, "Oh, Nancy, do you think you could buy us an ice cream?" It broke her heart to hear those words.

Though it was difficult seeing her family and friends struggling in poverty, Nancy was particularly upset by the official welcome she received when she arrived in Cuba. When she entered the airport in Cienfuegos, nervous and tired from the trip, a grim-faced state security officer hassled her with questions on how she had left and why she was coming back, and a customs officer then charged her $100 extra for the gifts she had brought. Fuming, Nancy told herself as she left the terminal that this was precisely what was wrong with the Cuban system. "Let's get out of here," she angrily told her mother and brother when she met them outside. Her frustration soon subsided as they rode home in an old Lada taxi, talking about what had happened at the airport.

Being with her family again after nearly twelve years compensated for the deep sadness that Nancy felt. She met her eight-year-old nephew and six-year-old niece, who warmed her heart when they called out, "*Tía Nancita.*" She brought them clothes, including Spiderman underwear for her nephew, and gave her video camera to her brother so that he could make home movies. She stocked her parents' house with supplies from cooking oil to toilet paper, and unloaded gifts from her suitcase ranging from shoes to vitamins. What she had brought quickly ran out. She had forgotten she had so many friends in Sagua la Grande.

But she was acutely aware that Cuba was no longer her home. She found herself explaining what a typical day was like in Miami and answering questions from friends who wondered if she had survived violent crimes of the sort they saw in American movies. She told them she had never been a victim and explained that her new life, though filled with hard work, was also rewarding and peaceful.

Some of Nancy's best friends threw a party for her, taking over a bar in the patio of a colonial house, where they talked and shared old photo albums. Her friends were engineers, doctors, and hotel workers. Many had married, some had divorced, and a number of them now had children. Nancy was overjoyed with the reunion and wished she could see her friends more often. But as she thought about them in the days that followed, she felt it was unjust for such capable, well-educated people to be stuck in low-paying state jobs with little hope of a different future. In the end, it seemed to Nancy that very little had changed since she left Sagua la Grande years before.

When it was time to leave, she kept her good-byes simple, planting kisses on the cheeks of her father and mother before slipping out the door with her brother for the airport. Nancy was glad she had gone to see her parents, though in the weeks after she left Cuba she was also filled with conflicting emotions.

"I want to be with them, but at the same time I don't want to be there with the situation that they're in today," she said. "It's so hard."

The experience had convinced Nancy that she did not want to return to the island for the foreseeable future. Yet in some ways she felt a new happiness and clarity at having returned to face her past. She acknowledged that her views had grown more strongly against the Cuban system over the years. Her one regret, she said, was that she hadn't left Cuba sooner.

"It bothers me, the loss of all that time of my life," she said during one of our conversations at her kitchen table. Nancy thought that if she had left when she was younger, she could have advanced a great deal more in her career. She recalled how she and Fico arrived with nothing and had to start their lives anew.

They hadn't been able to return to their old careers as engineers because doing so would require a great deal of study and time that they didn't have. Fico said he sometimes felt discouraged with his work as an electrician. Then again, they both felt thankful for what they had been able to achieve. Fico's son Franklin had followed them to the United States and enrolled in college. Nancy and Fico were steadily paying off their house, and Fico had bought a twenty-five-foot boat with his brother, sharing the monthly payments. He parked the boat trailer in the driveway and took the boat out on weekends to go snorkeling and spearfishing off the Keys. Fico was happy to have attained one of his dreams.

"It's incredible because in ten years we've achieved much more than what we could in more than thirty years in Cuba," Nancy said. She worked a second, part-time job as a paralegal on nights and weekends, typing information about immigration cases into a database on her laptop.

"It's a lot of work, but it also brings in money," she said cheerfully. The part-time job had helped her pay to remodel the house and make her trip to Cuba.

Nancy at home in Florida, 2005. (Ian James)

It irritated Nancy that her mother remained a staunch defender of the socialist system while at the same time receiving money from her and Fico to help make ends meet. One day during her mother's visit to Florida, the lights suddenly went out, and without thinking Nancy quipped, "Ay, Fidel's here." The room fell silent. Her mother chose to let the barb pass and didn't say a word in reply.

While Nancy shared her mother's view that the U.S. trade embargo was misguided, she strongly disagreed with the argument that the United States was to blame for Cuba's economic troubles. Fico faced similar disputes within his family. His adoptive father back in Cifuentes wrote to him saying he was hopeful about the future and didn't understand why Fico had decided to leave. Furious, Fico wrote back telling him to drop the lies because Cuba's political system was the root of all of their troubles.

Fico said he felt grateful to the United States and was glad to finally be applying for citizenship.

"For the rest of my years, I'm going to live in this country," he told me. "Cuba is a memory of the past." But he also said Cuba never leaves his mind.

"People in Cuba have no idea," he said. "The perception of people in Cuba is that we came here because of economic problems."

"In Cuba I ate a lot more lobster than I've eaten here in ten years, because I fished for it. It's not a problem of food," he said. "It's a problem of principles, it's a problem of moral values, of self-esteem, of feeling that you are a person."

Whenever he ate beef, Fico remembered friends and relatives on the island and thought about how they could seldom expect such a feast.

"People in Cuba think since you're in the U.S., you've got it made," he said. "They don't have any idea how much it hurts, how much this exile hurts."

Fico's eyes filled with tears.

"It hurts, it hurts," he said. "For me, Cuba hurts me every day of my life."

In the foothills of the Sierra del Escambray, rolling hills and cattle pastures passed in a blur outside the car window as Eloy shared memories of the lands where nearly half a century ago the Second Front had fought its war.

"We freed all of this," Eloy said, sweeping a hand across the mountains. "This was our territory."

In Trinidad, he stopped to visit Víctor Peña, a rebel soldier who had fought under his command. Eloy greeted him with a hearty hug and exclaimed, "¿Como estás, chico? You look good."

They traded memories of battles, including one in which Víctor was wounded in the leg and another in which Eloy reached down and hurled a grenade that had fallen short, just in time. "How is it possible that nothing about that history is written?" Víctor asked.

As we drove a winding road up into the mountains the next day, Eloy remembered how his troops had ambushed military convoys along the very same route, and how the rebels had eventually expanded their control across the entire Escambray. In one battle, they took the summit at Topes de Collantes, along with the military barracks, an armory, and a sanatorium for tuberculosis patients.

A steady rain was falling and clouds enveloped the summit as we approached. I asked Eloy how he felt to return. "The only thing in particular you remember is all the deaths there were in the fight against Batista in this area," Eloy said, growing somber. "And their sacrifice hasn't led to the freedoms that we fought for."

We stopped the car to pick up a hitchhiker, a seventy-five-year-old man who introduced himself as Mario León Martínez. He said he had lived his whole life in the Escambray.

"Do you know this area?" he asked Eloy.

"Yes, I spent a long time here as a rebel in the fight against Batista," Eloy replied.

They had been chatting for fifteen minutes by the time the hitchhiker asked Eloy his name.

"Aaaah, Gutiérrez Menoyo!" the old man said, chuckling. "So you were the chief then."

Eloy marveled at the surroundings as we passed through mist-shrouded pine forests. "There are places here that are priceless."

As we passed a hillside dotted with wild *mariposa* flowers, Eloy began to sing a verse from a song he wrote years ago upon his release from prison:

> *Traigo una flor que es de amor universal,*
> *una flor que hallé sangrando solitaria en un palmar.*
> *Su nombre es la mariposa, es nuestra flor nacional. . . .*

Eloy during a visit to the Sierra del Escambray, 2005. (Ian James)

Eloy had just turned seventy, but he insisted he still had plenty of life in him to battle for his principles and demand changes of the government.

"If they don't answer me, I'll keep insisting," he said. "Hope is never lost."

Shafts of sunlight danced across the hardwood floor at Paquito's house overlooking the Hudson River and Manhattan. On his mantel were arranged six Grammy awards, the golden phonographs all pointing the same direction. A seventh Grammy was missing: the one he had won years ago with Irakere. Here and there were reminders of Cuba—a large painting of royal palms, a photo of his father on the wall, and, in the garage, Paquito's 1957 Chevrolet Bel Air.

The twenty-five years since he left Cuba had been filled with success, allowing Paquito a comfortable life. There had been a great deal of hard work and occasional setbacks, such as a mild heart attack in 2002, but he had kept evolving and growing as a musician. I asked him what else he hoped to accomplish.

"The one achievement I would like is to be able to play in my country again. That's what I want," he answered, his words drifting between Spanish and English. "That's the only goal I have."

First the situation in Cuba would have to change, though. "I refuse to ask for a permit to enter my country. I don't accept that. It doesn't make any sense." He said it was a fundamental right for Cubans like him to be free to come and go, and added, "The day I can do that, I'll return."

He said he supposed that day would come only when Fidel Castro was gone. And what would he expect to see in post-Castro Cuba?

"Who knows? I don't have the slightest idea." Pausing to reflect, he

Paquito at home in New Jersey with his '57 Chevy, 2005. (Ian James)

Boys on the Malecón in Havana, 2001. (Ian James)

continued, "Nostalgia makes some things seem larger, it distorts the real image a lot from a distance. I would have to wait to get there, to see what has become of all this, the destruction they've left."

He said the hardest transitions for Cubans might be mentally adapting to a new system, like East Germans had done after the fall of the Berlin Wall. "The first problem is mental, how to adapt to the good and bad things of freedom."

He said living in exile had been difficult because "you don't belong to any place." Paquito loved New York, but during the cold winters he also dreamed of having an apartment on the Malecón to escape to. There was always something magical for him about that place where Havana met the sea, one of many images that kept Cuba alive in his mind.

"It's always there. I never left there. It's as if I'm visiting here, at least that's how I look at it," Paquito reflected, a tone of affection in his voice. "I never left."

Weekends at Nancy and Fico's house were a time to get together with friends and relatives for a meal of *lechón*, black beans and rice. They cleaned up the yard, roughhoused with their two German shepherds, and picked mangos or avocados. Sometimes Fico smoked a cigar on the porch.

Nancy's conflicted emotions often emerged when she took time to reflect on the Cuba she left behind. With sadness, she fretted about the situation of her parents and friends who remained there. She did not regret leaving Cuba. But at times, she also longed for the familiar and looked back fondly at that slower, simpler way of life.

"There are things about my country that I miss a lot, like when entering the province where I lived—it smelled of sugar cane. I've never noticed that here. Here the flowers don't smell," she explained. "There, flowers smell. And if you take a guava on the bus, everyone knows there is guava. But here, it just doesn't smell."

Tears came to her eyes as she spoke of lessons learned back home that she would never forget.

"We didn't really value money or material things. What matters is what's inside. And you know, I'm going to continue living like I did in Cuba. I have a dryer. But you see I still hang my clothes to dry on the line, because I like the smell it gets from the sun. You understand?" After a long silence she added, "That's Cuba, you know? I have my piece of Cuba here still."

Note on Sources

This book is based primarily on detailed interviews with Eloy Gutiérrez Menoyo, Paquito D'Rivera, Nancy Lledes, and others who have shared experiences with them. A list of those interviewed and named in the text appears among the notes. Recognizing that memory is imperfect, I have sought multiple sources whenever possible to confirm recollections of details or conversations. I have taken the liberty of using quote marks for past conversations or remarks that are recalled clearly by at least one person who was present.

I have generally used endnotes for written sources from which historical facts or quotes are drawn. In some limited cases, when various first-hand press accounts describe the same event, I have not attempted to cite each source individually when it would be cumbersome to sprinkle excessive endnotes throughout the text. For instance, the details of Castro's arrival in Havana in 1959 at the beginning of chapter 1 were collected through 1959 news accounts in the *New York Times*, the *Washington Post*, the *New York Herald Tribune*, the *Chicago Tribune*, and United Press International, plus various photographs of the rebels' arrival and some details from Robert E. Quirk's biography *Fidel Castro*.

I have drawn some quotations from personal letters or writings, and all relevant details about those sources are included in the text. I also have confirmed some quotations word for word through recordings of television footage and have not listed specific sources in those cases.

Other descriptions of places or historical events have been drawn from my travels in Cuba and the United States. For instance, a museum on Cuba's literacy campaign in Havana displayed uniforms worn by some volunteer teachers and Chinese-made kerosene lamps that were issued to the teachers.

The book progresses loosely in chronological order, though in some sections events have been placed slightly out of order in an effort to sustain the narratives.

People whose experiences appear in the book are identified by their real names or nicknames. A few have offered their memories or thoughts on the condition they not be identified, and in those cases I have left out their names.

Bibliography

SELECTED INTERVIEWS

Paquito D'Rivera
Eloy Gutiérrez Menoyo
Nancy Lledes

Cristóbal Díaz Ayala
Franco D'Rivera
Félix Durán
Nancy Espinosa Vergara
Federico Falcón
Brenda Feliciano
Carlos Franzetti
Félix Guerrero
Patricia Gutiérrez
Gladys Gutiérrez Menoyo
Rafael Huguet Sr.
Benjamín Lledes Aguila
Luis Lledes
Bruce Lundvall
Carlos Emilio Morales
Víctor Peña
Eneida Pérez-Méndez
Fernando Pruna
Roger Redondo
Enrique Rivera
Maura Rivera
Rosario Rivera

Alberto Romeu
Arnold Jay Smith
Dolores "Lolita" Torres Barrós
Dinorah Valdés
Raúl Valdés
Antonio Veciana

OTHER SOURCES

Alfonso, Pablo. "Cautela precedió viaje de Menoyo: Visita a Cuba se gestionó durante dos años." *El Nuevo Herald* (18 June 1995): 1A, 5A.

———. *Cuba, Castro y Los Católicos.* Miami: Ediciones Hispamerican Books, 1985.

———. "Menoyo habló 'de todo' con Castro." *El Nuevo Herald* (21 June 1995): 1A, 6A.

Anderson, Jon Lee. *Che Guevara: A Revolutionary Life.* New York: Grove Press, 1997.

Ardura, Rocío, and José Velez. "Menoyo: 'Fidel es un enfermo, un sádico, un hombre con auténtica afición por la mentira.'" Interview. *Hoja del Lunes* (12 Jan. 1987): 1–11.

Balmaseda, Liz. "Levantan huelga de hambre 96 presos en Cuba." *Miami Herald* (18 Dec. 1980): 2.

Bell, Maya, and Lynn Carrillo. "Marking a tragedy." *Sun-Sentinel* (9 July 1995): 1A.

Castañeda, Jorge G. *Compañero: The Life and Death of Che Guevara.* New York: Vintage Books, 1998.

Castro, Fidel. "Castro speech delivered in Ciudad Libertad." *Revolución* (9 Jan. 1959). Castro Speech Database, Latin American Network Information Center, University of Texas at Austin, www1.lanic.utexas.edu/la/cb/cuba/castro/1959/19590109.1 (19 Mar. 2005).

———. *La Invasión a Granada.* Mexico: Editorial Katún, 1983.

———. "Millones de manos inspiradas en el ejemplo del Che se extenderán para empuñar las armas." (Speech.) *Bohemia* no. 42, year 59 (20 Oct. 1967): 52–56, sup. 1–sup. 4.

"Castro at two landings." *The Associated Press* (14 Aug. 1959).

Chin, Paula, and Meg Grant. "Reunion: With help from his wife and his lover, jazzman Paquito D'Rivera gets back the son he left in Cuba." *People* (30 Jan. 1989): 94–96.

CIA Targets Fidel: Secret 1967 CIA Inspector General's Report on Plots to Assassinate Fidel Castro. Melbourne, Australia: Ocean Press, 1996.

Domingo, Alfredo Mateo. *Historia de la División Político-Administrativo de la Isla de Cuba (1607–1976)*. Havana: Editorial Arte y Literatura, 1977.

D'Rivera, Paquito. "Carta abierta a Fidel Castro." *Diario Las Americas* (21 Dec. 1988): 16A.

———. *Celebration*. Liner notes. CBS Records, 1988.

———. *Mi Vida Saxual*. San Juan, Puerto Rico: Editorial Plaza Mayor, 1999.

———. *Paquito Blowin'*. Liner notes. CBS Records, 1981.

———. "Rapsodia en blanco y negro." *El Nuevo Herald* (22 June 1987): 6.

Duff-Brown, Beth. "Cuban exile returns to island, brings out wife and children." *The Associated Press* (20 Dec. 1992).

"Fidel: 'Nazi hasta la medula.'" Interview with Eloy Gutiérrez Menoyo. *La Raza* (19–25 Feb. 1988): 1–2.

"A fighter with Castro: William Alexander Morgan." *New York Times* (15 Aug. 1959): 4.

Gayoso, Jay. "Ex-prisoner gets hero's welcome." *Miami Herald* (15 Mar. 1987): 1B.

Guevara, Ernesto Che. "A Sin of the Revolution." In *Episodes of the Cuban Revolutionary War 1956–58*, edited by Mary-Alice Waters, pp. 393–98. New York: Pathfinder, 1996.

Gutiérrez Menoyo, Eloy. *El Radarista*. Madrid: Editorial Playor, 1985.

———. "Paredón portatil." *Siempre de Miami* (17 Jan. 1972): 2.

———. "To the exile community: 'The whole world dialogues'—so why not Cubans?" *The Miami Herald* (27 Aug. 1993): 17A.

"Intervención del Comandante Ernesto Guevara en las Naciones Unidas." *Bohemia* no. 42, year 59 (20 Oct. 1967): 114.

Jeske, Lee. "Paquito D'Rivera: Alto in exile." *Down Beat* (Nov. 1983): 23–25.

Levine, Robert M. *Secret Missions to Cuba: Fidel Castro, Bernardo Benes, and Cuban Miami*. New York: Palgrave, 2001.

Mandel, Howard. "Paquito D'Rivera's freedom song." *Jazz Times* (May 1983): 10–12.

Meluza, Lourdes. "Castro frees foe after 21 years." *Miami Herald* (22 Dec. 1986): 1A.

Navarro, Mireya. "Castro confers with exiled foe." *New York Times* (28 June 1995): 1A.

———. "Last of refugees from Cuba in '94 flight now enter U.S." *New York Times* (1 Feb. 1996): 8A.

Newman, Maria. "10,000 marchers protest Manhattan rally to ease Cuba policy." *New York Times* (26 Jan. 1992): 24.

Nieto, Clara. *Masters of War: Latin America and U.S. Aggression from the Cuban Revolution through the Clinton Years*. New York: Seven Stories Press, 2003.

Ojito, Mirta. *Finding Mañana: A Memoir of a Cuban Exodus*. New York: Penguin, 2005.

Orihuela, Roberto. *Nunca Fui un Traidor: Retrato de un Farsante*. Havana: Editorial Capitán San Luis, 1991.

Pareles, Jon. "Havana to the Blue Note with Paquito D'Rivera." *New York Times* (23 May 1983).

Pérez, Louis A., Jr. *Cuba: Between Reform and Revolution*. New York: Oxford University Press, 1988.

Perez, Maribel. "Exiles planning protest flotilla to Cuban waters." *The Associated Press* (11 July 1995).

Pérez-Stable, Marifeli. *The Cuban Revolution: Origins, Course and Legacy*. 2d ed. New York: Oxford University Press, 1999.

Phillips, R. Hart. "Cubans capture invasion plane, accuse Trujillo." *New York Times* (15 Aug. 1959): 1, 4.

Potok, Mark. "Ex-rebel: Cuba revolution 'condemned.'" *Miami Herald* (23 Dec. 1986): 6A.

———. "Ex-rebel leader tells of horror in Castro jails." *Miami Herald* (25 Dec. 1986): 1A, 24A.

Quirk, Robert E. *Fidel Castro*. New York: W. W. Norton, 1993.

Raluy, Antonio. "Havana waterfront sealed off after worst anti-government riots." *Agence France Presse* (6 Aug. 1994).

Ramirez, Deborah. "Of Cuban bondage." *Sun-Sentinel* (3 July 1993): 1, 7D.

Rice, John. "Castro threatens to allow refugees to flood out." *The Associated Press* (5 Aug. 1994).

———. "Cuba describes deaths at sea, denies responsibility." *The Associated Press* (23 July 1994).

———. "Violence in Cuban capital; more Cubans flee." *The Associated Press* (5 Aug. 1994).

Reynaldo, Andres. "Un saxo en su lugar." *El Nuevo Día* (11 July 1982): 18–19.

Roig, Emma. "Eloy Gutiérrez Menoyo regresa a España tras permanecer preso 22 años en Cuba." *El País* (22 Dec. 1986): 15.

———. "Si hubiera conocido mejor a Castro me habría enfrentado con él mucho antes." *El País* (22 Dec. 1986): 16.

Santiago, Fabiola. "Old conspirators never die, they just keep politicking." *Miami Herald* Tropic (8 Oct. 1995): 6.

Severo, Richard. "U.S. cruise ship docks in Havana; Cuban-Americans stay aboard." *New York Times* (18 May 1977): A11.

Smith, Arnold Jay. "1st U.S. jazz gigs in 16 years." *Billboard* (4 June 1977): 1–18.

Snow, Anita. "Cuban activists predict a comeback for opposition after brutal battering." *The Associated Press* (6 July 2003).

————. "Cuban socialism now 'irrevocable' despite domestic, foreign challenges." *The Associated Press* (27 June 2002).

————. "Father of Elián González elected to Cuba's parliament." *The Associated Press* (23 Jan. 2003).

Szulc, Tad. *Fidel: A Critical Portrait.* New York: Avon Books / HarperCollins, 1986.

"Texto Completo del Interrogatorio Público Realizado Por Miembros del Departamento de Seguridad del Estado de la República de Cuba al Cabecilla Eloy Gutiérrez Menoyo y Otros Agentes Contrarrevolucionarios: Ramón Quesada Gómez, Domingo Ortega Acosta y Noel Salas Santos." Transcript (2 Feb. 1965): 1–16.

Thomas, Jo. *New York Times* (5 April–8 April 1980).

Tiegel, Eliot. "Cuba's Paquito D'Rivera: Irakere reedman eyes U.S. LP." *Billboard* (14 Apr. 1979): 35.

Valladares, Armando. *Against All Hope: The Prison Memoirs of Armando Valladares.* New York: Alfred A. Knopf, 1986.

Viera Trejo, Bernardo. "Humillación Trinidad: Hablan los hombres del II Frente del Escambray." *Bohemia* (23 Aug. 1959): 60–63, 112–13.

Winfield, Nicole. "Last Cuban refugees leave Guantánamo Naval Base." *The Associated Press* (31 Jan. 1996).

Wyden, Peter. *Bay of Pigs: The Untold Story.* New York: Simon and Schuster, 1979.

Zwerdling, Daniel. "More than 1,000 Cubans riot in Havana." Interview with Lionel Martin of the BBC. *All Things Considered* transcript. National Public Radio (6 Aug. 1994).

Notes

CHAPTER 1: HAVANA 1959

1. Fidel Castro, "Castro speech delivered in Ciudad Libertad," *Revolución*, 9 Jan. 1959, Castro Speech Database, Latin American Network Information Center, University of Texas at Austin, www1.lanic.utexas.edu/la/cb/cuba/castro/1959/1959 0109.1 (19 Mar. 2005).

2. Robert E. Quirk, *Fidel Castro* (New York: W. W. Norton, 1993), 221.

3. Castro, "Castro speech delivered in Ciudad Libertad."

4. Louis A. Pérez Jr., *Cuba: Between Reform and Revolution* (New York: Oxford University Press, 1988), 320–21.

5. Paquito D'Rivera, *Mi Vida Saxual* (San Juan, Puerto Rico: Editorial Plaza Mayor, 1999), 67.

6. Quirk, *Fidel Castro*, 301–2.

7. Pérez, *Cuba: Between Reform*, 325–26.

8. Clara Nieto, *Masters of War: Latin America and U.S. Aggression from the Cuban Revolution through the Clinton Years* (New York: Seven Stories Press, 2003), 73–76.

9. Tad Szulc, *Fidel: A Critical Portrait* (New York: Avon Books / HarperCollins, 1986), 547.

10. Szulc, *Fidel: A Critical Portrait*, 547.

11. Szulc, *Fidel: A Critical Portrait*, 549.

12. Peter Wyden, *Bay of Pigs: The Untold Story* (New York: Simon and Schuster, 1979), 219–20.

13. Quirk, *Fidel Castro*, 374.

CHAPTER 2: A MUSICAL BOY, A BEACH IDYLL, A REBEL PLOT

1. Bernardo Viera Trejo, "Humillación Trinidad: Hablan los hombres del II Frente del Escambray," *Bohemia*, 23 Aug. 1959, 60–62.

2. "Castro at two landings," *The Associated Press*, 14 Aug. 1959.

3. Viera Trejo, "Humillación Trinidad," 112.

4. R. Hart Phillips, "Cubans capture invasion plane, accuse Trujillo," *New York Times*, 15 Aug. 1959, 1.

5. Ernesto "Che" Guevara, "A Sin of the Revolution," in *Episodes of the Cuban Revolutionary War 1956–58*, ed. Mary-Alice Waters (New York: Pathfinder, 1996), 394–96.

6. "Texto Completo del Interrogatorio Público Realizado Por Miembros del Departamento de Seguridad del Estado de la República de Cuba al Cabecilla Eloy Gutiérrez Menoyo y Otros Agentes Contrarrevolucionarios: Ramón Quesada Gómez, Domingo Ortega Acosta y Noel Salas Santos," Transcript, 2 Feb. 1965, 1.

7. "Texto Completo del Interrogatorio Público," 1–16.

8. Armando Valladares, *Against All Hope: The Prison Memoirs of Armando Valladares* (New York: Alfred A. Knopf, 1986), 196.

CHAPTER 3: SCHOOL, ARMY, JAIL

1. Louis A. Pérez Jr., *Cuba: Between Reform and Revolution* (New York: Oxford University Press, 1988), 358–59.

2. Paquito D'Rivera, *Mi Vida Saxual* (San Juan, Puerto Rico: Editorial Plaza Mayor, 1999), 117.

3. Robert E. Quirk, *Fidel Castro* (New York: W. W. Norton, 1993), 135.

CHAPTER 4: REVOLUTIONARIES, "MODERN MUSIC," HAVANA NIGHTS

1. "Intervención del Comandante Ernesto Guevara en las Naciones Unidas," *Bohemia*, no. 42, year 59, 20 Oct. 1967, 114.

2. Clara Nieto, *Masters of War: Latin America and U.S. Aggression from the Cuban Revolution through the Clinton Years* (New York: Seven Stories Press, 2003), 153.

3. Jorge G. Castañeda, *Compañero: The Life and Death of Che Guevara* (New York: Vintage Books, 1998), 391–401.

4. Jon Lee Anderson, *Che Guevara: A Revolutionary Life* (New York: Grove Press, 1997), 741. Also *New York Times*, 20 Oct. 1967.

5. Paquito D'Rivera, *Mi Vida Saxual* (San Juan, Puerto Rico: Editorial Plaza Mayor, 1999), 138–39.

6. Fidel Castro, "Millones de manos inspiradas en el ejemplo del Che se extenderán para empuñar las armas" (speech), *Bohemia*, no. 42, year 59, 20 Oct. 1967, 52–56, sup. 1–sup. 4.

7. D'Rivera, *Mi Vida Saxual*, 166.

8. D'Rivera, *Mi Vida Saxual*, 198–99.

CHAPTER 5: BLOODSHED, LETTERS HOME, A LOVE AFFAIR

1. Ernesto "Che" Guevara, "A Sin of the Revolution," in *Episodes of the Cuban Revolutionary War 1956–58*, ed. Mary-Alice Waters (New York: Pathfinder, 1996), 394.

2. "A fighter with Castro: William Alexander Morgan," *New York Times*, 15 Aug. 1959, 4.

3. Robert E. Quirk, *Fidel Castro* (New York: W. W. Norton, 1993), 634–35.

4. Quirk, *Fidel Castro*, 642.

5. *CIA Targets Fidel: Secret 1967 CIA Inspector General's Report on Plots to Assassinate Fidel Castro* (Melbourne, Australia: Ocean Press, 1996), 77.

6. Paquito D'Rivera, *Mi Vida Saxual* (San Juan, Puerto Rico: Editorial Plaza Mayor, 1999), 178–79.

CHAPTER 6: RAZORS, RELIGION, COMMUNIST YOUTH

1. Eloy Gutiérrez Menoyo, "Paredón portatil," *Siempre de Miami*, 17 Jan. 1972, 2.

2. Pablo M. Alfonso, *Cuba, Castro y Los Católicos* (Miami: Ediciones Hispamerican Books, 1985), 104–6.

3. Tad Szulc, *Fidel: A Critical Portrait* (New York: Avon Books / HarperCollins, 1986), 470.

4. Louis A. Pérez Jr., *Cuba: Between Reform and Revolution* (New York: Oxford University Press, 1988), 358–59.

5. Alfredo Mateo Domingo, *Historia de la División Político-Administrativo de la Isla de Cuba (1607–1976)* (Havana: Editorial Arte y Literatura, 1977), 83.

CHAPTER 7: A JAZZ CRUISE, A MOUNTAIN HIKE, A PRISON TALE

1. Robert M. Levine, *Secret Missions to Cuba: Fidel Castro, Bernardo Benes, and Cuban Miami* (New York: Palgrave, 2001), 89.

2. Levine, *Secret Missions*, 95.

3. Richard Severo, "U.S. cruise ship docks in Havana; Cuban-Americans stay aboard," *New York Times*, 18 May 1977, A11.

4. Arnold Jay Smith, "1st U.S. jazz gigs in 16 years," *Billboard*, 4 June 1977, 1–18.

5. Mark Potok, "Ex-rebel leader tells of horror in Castro jails," *Miami Herald*, 25 Dec. 1986, 24A.

6. Levine, *Secret Missions*, 114–15.

7. Levine, *Secret Missions*, 116.

8. Levine, *Secret Missions*, 118–130.

9. Eloy Gutiérrez Menoyo, *El Radarista* (Madrid: Editorial Playor, 1985), 17.

10. Gutiérrez Menoyo, *El Radarista*, 19–95.

11. Author's note: Cuban music historian Cristóbal Díaz Ayala told me he is quite certain, after many years of research, that Irakere's U.S. album marked the first time since the 1959 revolution that musicians living in Cuba had recorded an album in the United States.

12. Eliot Tiegel, "Cuba's Paquito D'Rivera: Irakere reedman eyes U.S. LP," *Billboard*, 14 Apr. 1979, 35.

CHAPTER 8: MARIEL

1. Jo Thomas, *New York Times*, 5 April–8 April 1980.

2. Mirta Ojito, *Finding Mañana: A Memoir of a Cuban Exodus* (New York: Penguin, 2005), 100–101.

3. Ojito, *Finding Mañana*, 104; Thomas, *New York Times*, 5 April–8 April 1980.

4. Thomas, *New York Times*, 6 April–7 April 1980.

5. Robert E. Quirk, *Fidel Castro* (New York: W. W. Norton, 1993), 807–8.

6. Paquito D'Rivera, *Mi Vida Saxual* (San Juan, Puerto Rico: Editorial Plaza Mayor, 1999), 227.

7. Jon Pareles, "Havana to the Blue Note with Paquito D'Rivera," *New York Times*, 23 May 1983.

CHAPTER 9: NEW YORK CITY, CAMPUS LIFE, A HUNGER STRIKE

1. Paquito D'Rivera, *Paquito Blowin'*, liner notes, CBS Records, 1981.

2. Andres Reynaldo, "Un saxo en su lugar," *El Nuevo Día*, 11 July 1982, 18–19.

3. Robert E. Quirk, *Fidel Castro* (New York: W. W. Norton, 1993), 822.

4. Fidel Castro, *La Invasión a Granada* (Mexico: Editorial Katún, 1983), 41–60.

5. Liz Balmaseda, "Levantan huelga de hambre 96 presos en Cuba," *Miami Herald*, 18 Dec. 1980, 2.

CHAPTER 10: CUBAN DOMINOES, THE LONG WAIT, FREEDOM

1. Howard Mandel, "Paquito D'Rivera's freedom song," *Jazz Times*, May 1983, 10.

2. Mandel, "Paquito D'Rivera's freedom song," 12.

3. Jon Pareles, "Havana to the Blue Note with Paquito D'Rivera," *New York Times*, 23 May 1983.

4. Lee Jeske, "Paquito D'Rivera: Alto in exile," *Down Beat*, Nov. 1983, 24.

5. Mark Potok, "Ex-rebel leader tells of horror in Castro jails," *Miami Herald*, 25 Dec. 1986, 1A.

6. Lourdes Meluza, "Castro frees foe after 21 years," *Miami Herald*, 22 Dec. 1986, 1A.

7. Meluza, "Castro frees foe," 1A, 18A.

8. Emma Roig, "Eloy Gutiérrez Menoyo regresa a España tras permanecer preso 22 años en Cuba," *El País*, 22 Dec. 1986, 15.

9. Emma Roig, "Si hubiera conocido mejor a Castro me habría enfrentado con él mucho antes," *El País*, 22 Dec. 1986, 16.

10. Mark Potok, "Ex-rebel: Cuba revolution 'condemned,'" *Miami Herald*, 23 Dec. 1986, 6A.

11. Jay Gayoso, "Ex-prisoner gets hero's welcome," *Miami Herald*, 15 Mar. 1987, 1B.

12. Fabiola Santiago, "Old conspirators never die, they just keep politicking," *Miami Herald*, Tropic, 8 Oct. 1995, 6.

CHAPTER 11: WEARINESS, A REUNION, SPEAKING OUT

1. Paquito D'Rivera, *Celebration*, liner notes, CBS Records, 1988.

2. Paquito D'Rivera, "Carta abierta a Fidel Castro," *Diario Las Americas*, 21 Dec. 1988, 16A.

3. Paula Chin and Meg Grant, "Reunion: With help from his wife and his lover, jazzman Paquito D'Rivera gets back the son he left in Cuba," *People*, 30 Jan. 1989, 94–96.

4. Chin and Grant, "Reunion."

5. Rocío Ardura and José Velez, "Menoyo: 'Fidel es un enfermo, un sádico, un hombre con auténtica afición por la mentira,'" *Hoja del Lunes*, 12 Jan. 1987, 1–11.

6. "Fidel: 'Nazi hasta la medula,'" *La Raza*, 19–25 Feb. 1988, 1–2.

7. Roberto Orihuela, *Nunca Fui un Traidor: Retrato de un Farsante* (Havana: Editorial Capitán San Luis, 1991), 12, 128–30. Author's note: To check on claims of a relationship between Eloy and the CIA, I submitted a letter to the agency under the Freedom of Information Act (FOIA) requesting records that mentioned his name or that of Alpha 66 between 1957 and 1965. The FOIA request turned up ninety-four documents totaling 243 pages. Those documents, many with blacked-out portions, showed that the CIA closely followed Eloy's efforts in the early 1960s to raise money and carry out attacks on the Cuban coast and on merchant ships. None of the documents, however, pointed to a collaborative relationship between Eloy and the CIA. One cable mentioned that some of Eloy's detractors noted a "pink," or lightly communist, tinge to his views.

CHAPTER 12: BOAT PEOPLE

1. Deborah Ramirez, "Of Cuban bondage," *Sun-Sentinel*, 3 July 1993, 1, 7D.

2. Eloy Gutiérrez Menoyo, "To the exile community: 'The whole world dialogues'—so why not Cubans?" *The Miami Herald*, 27 Aug. 1993, 17A.

3. Beth Duff-Brown, "Cuban exile returns to island, brings out wife and children," *The Associated Press*, 20 Dec. 1992.

4. Maria Newman, "10,000 marchers protest Manhattan rally to ease Cuba policy," *New York Times*, 26 Jan. 1992, 24.

5. Paquito D'Rivera, "Rapsodia en blanco y negro," *El Nuevo Herald*, 22 June 1987, 6.

6. Marifeli Pérez-Stable, *The Cuban Revolution: Origins, Course and Legacy*, 2d ed. (New York: Oxford University Press, 1999), 174–76.

7. Maribel Perez, "Exiles planning protest flotilla to Cuban waters," *The Associated Press*, 11 July 1995.

8. Maya Bell and Lynn Carrillo, "Marking a tragedy," *Sun-Sentinel*, 9 July 1995, 1A.

9. John Rice, "Cuba describes deaths at sea, denies responsibility," *The Associated Press*, 23 July 1994.

10. Daniel Zwerdling, "More than 1,000 Cubans riot in Havana," interview with Lionel Martin of the BBC, *All Things Considered* transcript, National Public Radio, 6 Aug. 1994.

11. Antonio Raluy, "Havana waterfront sealed off after worst anti-government riots," *Agence France Presse*, 6 Aug. 1994.

12. Zwerdling, "More than 1,000 Cubans."

13. Raluy, "Havana waterfront sealed off."

14. John Rice, "Violence in Cuban capital; more Cubans flee," and "Castro threatens to allow refugees to flood out," *The Associated Press*, 5 Aug. 1994.

CHAPTER 13: GUANTÁNAMO

1. Nicole Winfield, "Last Cuban refugees leave Guantánamo Naval Base," *The Associated Press*, 31 Jan. 1996.

2. Mireya Navarro, "Last of refugees from Cuba in '94 flight now enter U.S.," *New York Times*, 1 Feb. 1996, 8A.

CHAPTER 14: FACING CASTRO

1. Anita Snow, "Father of Elián González elected to Cuba's parliament," *The Associated Press*, 23 Jan. 2003.

2. Pablo Alfonso, "Cautela precedió viaje de Menoyo: Visita a Cuba se gestionó durante dos años," *El Nuevo Herald*, 18 June 1995, 1A, 5A.

3. Fabiola Santiago, "Old conspirators never die, they just keep politicking," *Miami Herald*, Tropic, 8 Oct. 1995, 6.

4. Santiago, "Old conspirators."

5. Mireya Navarro, "Castro confers with exiled foe," *New York Times*, 28 June 1995, 1A.

6. Pablo Alfonso, "Menoyo habló 'de todo' con Castro," *El Nuevo Herald*, 21 June 1995, 1A, 6A.

CHAPTER 15: EXILE

1. Anita Snow, "Cuban socialism now 'irrevocable' despite domestic, foreign challenges," *The Associated Press*, 27 June 2002.

2. Anita Snow, "Cuban activists predict a comeback for opposition after brutal battering," *The Associated Press*, 6 July 2003.

Index

About the Author

Ian Michael James is a journalist who has written extensively about Latin America as a correspondent for The Associated Press. He became deeply interested in Cuba and the personal stories of its émigrés while working as a reporter in Miami in the late 1990s, when he traveled to the island and began learning about Cubans' experiences both in their homeland and in the United States. Originally from California, he learned Spanish in his youth during a summer spent with workers on a cattle ranch in Guatemala, where he began documenting people's lives through writing and photography. A graduate of Duke and Stanford universities, he has written for newspapers including the *St. Petersburg Times* and the *Los Angeles Times*. In his many reporting assignments for the AP, in places from the Caribbean to the Middle East, he has been particularly interested in telling the human stories behind larger social and political trends. He currently lives in Venezuela, where he is the AP's bureau chief.